ARCHAEOLOGY

AT MONTICELLO

Monticello Archaeology

1979–1991

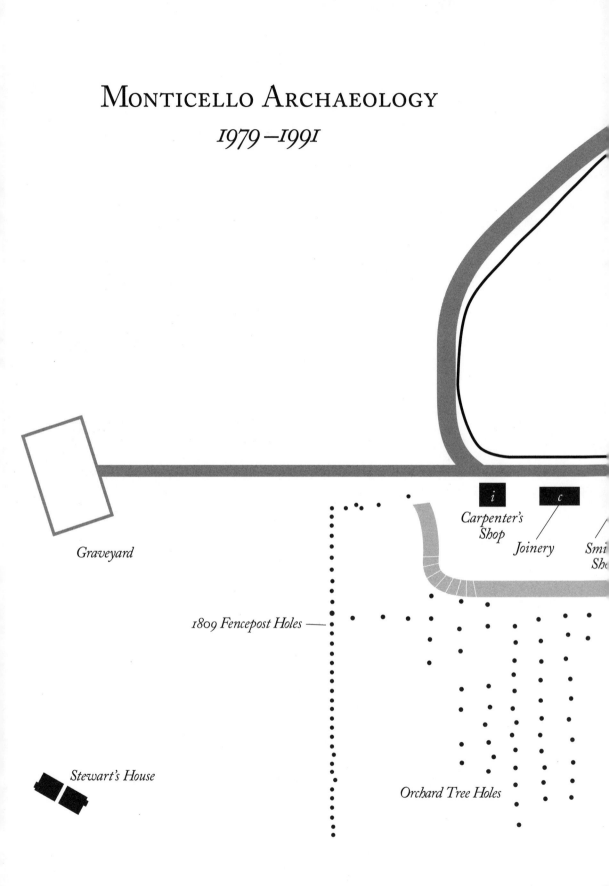

Graveyard

Carpenter's Shop

Joinery

Smi Sho

1809 Fencepost Holes —

Stewart's House

Orchard Tree Holes

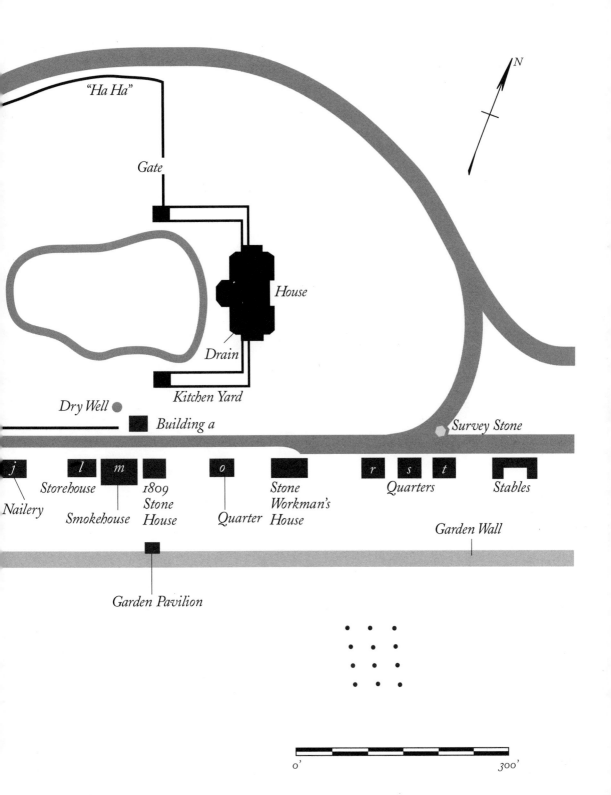

"Ha Ha"

Gate

House

Drain

Kitchen Yard

Dry Well

Building a

Survey Stone

j
Nailery

Storehouse

l   *m*
Smokehouse

1809
Stone
House

o
Quarter

Stone
Workman's
House

r   *s*   *t*
Quarters

Stables

Garden Wall

Garden Pavilion

N

0'   300'

ARCHAEOLOGY

AT MONTICELLO

Artifacts of Everyday Life
in the Plantation Community

William M. Kelso

Preface by James Deetz

THOMAS JEFFERSON MEMORIAL FOUNDATION
Monticello Monograph Series

THE THOMAS JEFFERSON MEMORIAL FOUNDATION, INC.

This publication was made possible by a gift from Luella and Martin Davis.

CONTENTS

Preface

*W*hen William M. Kelso initiated the program of archaeology at Monticello in 1979, his work was held in the highest regard by his colleagues in historical archaeology, particularly with respect to his five-year investigation of the Kingsmill Plantations. His field procedures have always produced excavations which are models of order and precision. His "before and after" photographs of the half-cellared house at Kingsmill's utopia set a standard which has been emulated countless times by archaeologists working in the Chesapeake and elsewhere. These meticulous excavation techniques were to figure significantly when Kelso first encountered the red clay soils of Albemarle County.

Yet, at the time that Kelso initiated his Monticello research, one could not help but wonder what archaeology could add to the Jeffersonian story. This was the kind of archaeology that many of us questioned, in that it dealt with a literate elite about whom the written record would be most eloquent. As Henry Glassie writes in *Folk Housing in Middle Virginia:* "A knowledge of Thomas Jefferson might be based on his writings and only supplemented by study of Monticello, but for most people, such as the folks who were chopping farms out of the woods a few miles to the east while Jefferson was writing at his desk, the procedure must be reversed" (1975: 12). Kelso's twelve years of excavations at Monticello have demonstrated amply that there were things to be learned about Jefferson that were not to be found in his copious writings, as well as about other members of the Monticello community who had more in common with the "folks who were chopping farms out of the woods" than with the great man himself.

When excavations were begun at Monticello in 1979, Jefferson's nineteenth-century landscape was only a palimpsest, overlain and in places erased by subsequent filling, grading, and planting. The first phase of Kelso's excavations at Monticello was directed at the recovery of the landscape as Jefferson had developed it during his lifetime. The results were nothing less than spectacular, and a good portion of the original fence lines, walls, and plantings of various kinds were exposed and formed the basis of what the visitor sees today upon visiting

Monticello. The undertaking was a very ambitious one, on a scale rarely if ever encountered before in historical archaeology. True, as reported in the introduction, modest efforts at investigating the grounds immediately adjacent to the houses were undertaken at Kingsmill and Carter's Grove, but these do not begin to approach the landscape archaeology at Monticello. Indeed, it can be fairly said that Monticello saw the birth of landscape archaeology as we know it today. The first full book on the subject, *Earth Patterns*, published in 1990 and edited by Kelso and Rachel Most, grew out of the Monticello landscape research.

In the course of excavations, literally thousands of feet of garden walls and fence lines were defined. In the latter instance, an ability to read soil stain patterns was critical. Kelso's careful and meticulous experience in the Chesapeake enabled him to define the faintest of soil stains under very difficult circumstances. In fact, there were those of us who felt it was impossible to see soil stains in the red Albemarle clay. But Kelso was able to do it and do it well. One of the more impressive efforts involved in the landscape research was the excavation of Jefferson's orchard, evidenced by regularly spaced planting holes for trees. In this instance, the written record was an important adjunct to the archaeology, since it specified the spacing of the trees which matched the intervals between the soil stains marking the location of the planting holes. This agreement between documents and archaeology raises another point. Records and archaeology do not always confirm each other. At Monticello, Jefferson planned and usually executed various landscape projects. But in some cases, the archaeology shows that idealized plans were not always realized. Furthermore, the Monticello landscape did not appear in its fully developed state. Rather it grew in increments, and in some cases, certain features, such as fences, were modified or replaced. It is in this case that the archaeology was of critical importance. The construction of this or that fence line could be dated by artifacts found in the post holes, enabling a sequence of remodeling and new construction to be carefully developed.

A conspicuous feature of the landscape of Monticello was Mulberry Row, a line of shops and residences to the south between the house and the garden wall. By the twentieth century, only two of the original structures still stood; all of the others had vanished. A line of building foundations was uncovered as a part of the landscape archaeology, since a fence line defined by several hundred feet of post holes regularly encountered the footings of these buildings. Nine of them were used to house slaves. While these people were domestic slaves, the field hands being housed at a greater remove from the house, we must not see them as forming an undifferentiated population. On the contrary, the archaeology shows that in terms of both housing and material possessions there was considerable variation. The archaeology further demonstrates that over time Jefferson made an effort to improve the quality of housing of all the Mulberry Row residents. Excavation of the other buildings on Mulberry Row provided important insights regarding a number of plantation industries. Kelso has referred to Mulberry Row as "Main Street, Monticello," and the name seems quite appropriate.

In the concluding chapter of the book, we are given an appreciation of the richness and diversity of the material objects unearthed during the twelve years of archaeology at Monticello. What is particularly striking about this section, and particularly the epilogue, is the sensitivity to the emotional quality that these artifacts possess. Not mere objects, but things that were owned, used and undoubtedly cherished in some cases, they form a palpable link to the past. From the microscope parts found near the house to the tin cup possibly made by Isaac, a slave artisan, we sense the vibrancy of another time, now vanished, but still with us in the recovered landscape, buildings, and myriad objects.

—James Deetz
University of Virginia

Prologue

Thomas Jeffferson: Archaeologist

He could barely see them through the wispy morning fog, but their quiet gait and towering silhouettes told him there was something different about these riders. Indians! The freckled, auburn-haired boy leaped from the steps of his faded frame farm house and sprinted down the hill toward them, fearing that he might miss a closer view of what he thought were warriors. He had so far known Indians only secondhand, through the vivid stories told by his father, Peter, the frontier surveyor.

The year was 1751; the place, Shadwell, Albemarle County, Virginia; and the boy, Thomas Jefferson, future author of the Declaration of Independence and third president of the United States. That day Jefferson was only an inquisitive boy of eight who had his undivided attention focused on the curious road travelers. From the shadow of the massive sycamore Jefferson got his first close look at these native Americans as they made their way back to their land beyond the nearby Blue Ridge Mountains from meetings with the Royal Governor at the capitol in Williamsburg. He counted twenty braves as they passed, their silver or jet black hair sorting the warriors from the sages.

After they passed, the young observer decided to follow along at a respectful distance. When they reached the Rivanna at the base of Pantops Mountain, they suddenly turned off the main road to follow the meandering river. Soon the river forked and they followed the south branch just as Tom had heard they would, until they came to an ancient cleared field. There the riders dismounted and reverently approached a large earthen mound.

The boy wondered about the power the mound seemed to have over the Indians and wanted to take a closer look. But the hour was growing late. He knew his father had farm work enough for him back at Shadwell, and Thomas Jefferson was never one to stay clear of his school work for long. It was, however, that first brief look at Indians and his inexhaustible appetite for learning that would eventually compel the young scholar to uncover the secret of the earthen mound.

Though the details of this account are imaginary, the encounter did happen. In 1781 Jefferson wrote in his book, *Notes on the State of Virginia*, "about thirty years ago" an Indian party strayed some "half a dozen" miles off the main road to gather and express "sorrow" at a mound.[1] If Jefferson himself witnessed this pilgrimage, then he would have been eight years old at the time (he was 38 years old in 1781). It is certain that Jefferson, at some time in his twenties, organized an archaeological expedition to that mound, directed archaeological fieldwork, analyzed what he found, and published his conclusions. Archaeologists today agree that his work earned him the title of the first American archaeologist, the first archaeologist to engage in true problem-oriented research. There would be no comparable work for another sixty years.

It is somehow both fitting and ironic that the very principles and methods first used by Thomas Jefferson in the eighteenth century are used today in the twentieth century to study the material world of Jefferson. The main chapters of this book describe that study and give meaning to Jefferson's world. But before that account, it seems appropriate here to review just what it was that Jefferson first discovered about doing archaeology (i.e., his archaeological process) which in turn explains how we are able to sort through the soil at Monticello and find and identify remains that were left there during Jefferson's lifetime.

During the summer of 1780 the secretary of the French legation to America in Philadelphia, François Marbois, circulated a questionnaire concerning the American states to a number of the members of the Continental Congress. Joseph Jones, member from Virginia, sent his questionnaire along to the person that many had learned to recognize as the man most likely to have the answers— Thomas Jefferson, Governor of Virginia. Jefferson spent the next year, especially the time during which he was recuperating from a sprained wrist at Poplar Forest, his retreat plantation, writing out answers to a number of Marbois' questions. He never intended to publish these notes but for various reasons and at various times they got into print during the 1780s and 1790s.

Chapter XI of Jefferson's *Notes on the State of Virginia* describes the aborigines of Virginia including tribe names, languages, population, and distribution. It was in this chapter that Jefferson described the archaeological excavation of the mound that is located on the banks of the south branch of the Rivanna River about five miles north of modern Charlottesville. The research process he describes includes most of the basic procedures archaeologists follow today.

Before the fieldwork, Jefferson first discussed the theories concerning the nature of the mound and in true scientific fashion cast them as three hypothetical scenarios to test with excavation. These included:

1. [the mounds contained only] " ... bones of those who were fallen in battle"
2. [the mounds contained a collection] " ... at certain periods the bones of all their dead"
3. [the mounds were] "general sepulchre[s] for towns [each buried leaning together]"[2]

He next devised his strategy for excavation beginning with test holes:

> I first dug superficially in several parts of it [the mound] and came to collections of bones ... lying in utmost confusion ... to give the idea of bones emptied promiscuously from a bag or basket.[3]

Then Jefferson decided to dig a cross-section trench through the mound and thereby discovered the relationship of soil layers to time:

> I proceeded to make a perpendicular cut through the body of the barrow, that I might examine its internal structure ... opened to the former surface of the earth ... at one end of the section were four strata of bone plainly distinguishable; at the other, three; the strata in one part not ranging with the other.[4]

This firmly establishes Jefferson's understanding of the inter-relationship of soil layer build-up through time and the importance of the context of the artifacts, in this case human bones. It is from this evidence that he then goes on to arrive at the most logical explanation of the use of the mound:

It [the mound] has derived both origin and growth from the accustomary collection of bones and deposition together [because of]:

1. the number of bones,

2. their confused position,

3. their being in different strata,

4. the strata in one part having no correspondence with those of another,

5. different states of decay in these strata … indicates a difference in time of inhumation,

6. the existence of infant bones.[5]

Thus, Thomas Jefferson came to understand that Indians customarily buried collections of bones periodically. That means that through excavation and analysis, Jefferson learned something about human behavior—the ultimate goal of archaeology. The soil and the artifacts are but a means to an end. He also shows us quite clearly that archaeology is a step-by-step process where the specifics of the excavation and careful observation of the relationships of artifacts to soil are the key to conclusions. He would never allow fast forwarding to sweeping generalities about human existence. It was important to Jefferson to determine the particular facts about one mound and to make conclusions about that mound. It is implied that what the one mound had to say *might* be true for others nearby but we can also assume that he would have others field examined before making broadstroke conclusions about Indian mortuary practices. Archaeology at Monticello took heed of that caution.

Of course, beyond his archaeological bent, it is an understatement to say that Thomas Jefferson was a remarkably unique and talented man. But precisely what he accomplished that most proves his genius is the subject of much debate. Many who know the building and landscape of his Virginia mountaintop home, Monticello, would argue that Jefferson's architectural and landscape designs were foremost among his many achievements. Indeed, it was at Monticello in 1769 that the fledgling architect began the more than one-half century campaign to convert his *little mountain* into what many critics recognize as one of America's most sophisticated architectural and landscape designs.

Creating that living space on a mountain was not easy; lack of water and access to the hilltop were constant problems, as was modification of the sloping ground to plant gardens, orchards, vineyards, and build dependent buildings and roadways. All of this wrought engineering problems of no small consequence. But bit by bit, Jefferson's years of effort to create his rural estate left a heavy imprint on the Monticello landscape. The Monticello development campaign began in 1767 with the leveling of the mountaintop to create the platform for the house and its supporting village of outbuildings along the approach road he called Mulberry Row, and ended in 1814 with the completion of the subterranean moat-like barrier surrounding the west lawn known as a ha-ha. (Usually a fence hidden in a ditch to create an uninterrupted picturesque vista, the word ha-ha comes from the Latin meaning hedge.)

As vital as it was to the success of the mansion, Jefferson's landscape design had become only dimly visible and was in some cases completely gone by the time the Thomas Jefferson Memorial Foundation was formed (1923) to "hold, preserve and maintain Monticello as a national memorial." Repair and conservation of the house, basic maintenance of the landscape, and finding a way to pay the mortgage were the immediate concerns of the newly formed Monticello preservation group. Consequently, no major restoration work was attempted on the landscape for years except for the creative effort of the Garden Club of Virginia to redesign the west lawn garden in 1939. But by the late 1970s, the house restoration program was complete enough to shift its attention to the landscape. The survival of detailed plans and notes in Jefferson's hand of the road system, roadside plantings, layout of the vegetable garden, orchards, vineyards, and specifications for scores of ancillary buildings including a decorative garden pavilion, craft shops, slave quarters, and utilitarian outbuildings rendered the prospects of accurately redefining the lost Jefferson Monticello landscape exceptionally bright. Elsewhere in Virginia the success of the archaeological landscape research at Carter's Grove and Kingsmill plantations and the maturing of the process of historical archaeology suggested that archaeological study could aid in the restoration of Monticello, especially when conducted in concert with these unusually complete Jefferson drawings and specifications. Consequently, in June 1979, archaeological excavations began to define Monticello's designed landscape. Further work over the next decade (1980-1989) along the domestic and light commercial area known as Mulberry Row uncovered the remains of houses, shops, storage buildings, a garden paling fence and pavilion, buildings in the south kitchen yard of the house and terraced gardens, orchards and vineyards.

This book describes and interprets these archaeological discoveries. A summary documentary history of the development of Jefferson's Monticello follows in an attempt to create an historical context for the archaeological discussion. This is followed by a discussion of the landscape surrounding Monticello. Chapter 3 provides insight into Mulberry Row and slave life. And Chapter 4, Things of Everyday Life, provides further insight into the everyday objects that were part of Jefferson's life. These objects were selected as representative of collections from archaeological features having relatively precise dates of deposit and/or associations with the Jefferson family or the slave community. The cost of illustrating or publishing even a list of the thousands of artifacts recovered in the excavation is prohibitive. One can only hope that the representative objects chosen for illustration impartially reflect the daily lives of a cross section of the Monticello population, and that they will be useful to researchers doing comparative archaeological site analysis in the future.

ENDNOTES

[1] T. Jefferson, *Notes on the State of Virginia*, ed. William Peden (Chapel Hill: University of North Carolina Press, 1955), 100.

[2] Ibid., pp. 97-98.

[3] Ibid., p. 98.

[4] Ibid., p. 99.

[5] Ibid., p. 100.

Chapter One

Thomas Jefferson's Monticello

*W*hen Thomas Jefferson reached the age of twenty, he inherited from his father, Peter, the approximately 7,000 acres in central Virginia (near the future town of Charlottesville) that became known as Monticello. Peter Jefferson first patented the land which he called Shadwell in 1735 and probably began living there two years before Thomas was born (April 13, 1743). While Thomas spent much of his first two decades away at school, and five years in residence with his family at Tuckahoe Plantation near Richmond, he settled at Shadwell with his mother and sisters during his early law career. During those years he formulated his plans to eventually occupy the small mountain that stood on the Shadwell horizon nearby. Indeed, Monticello would become the primary object of most of his creative genius and domestic life thereafter.

By 1767 he began employing some of the over fifty slave laborers he had inherited from his father in leveling a rectangle on the crest of the mountain for his house. In 1770, the year a fire destroyed the Shadwell house and his library and early papers, Jefferson finished the first structure on the mountaintop, the South Pavilion. Thereafter Jefferson used the pavilion as his domestic quarters as he directed the ongoing construction of his Monticello home.

During the Revolutionary War, Jefferson's attention was turned from building his house to building the nation, so progress was slow until he retired from the governorship of Virginia in 1781. Nevertheless, the first of two versions of Monticello, a very different one from the famous domed style so familiar today, took shape featuring two-story columned porticos. As rooms were finished the family moved in even with construction still in full swing in other sections of their house. As construction advanced, each public room was decorated with a different classical order, but little of this scheme was completed when the house was enlarged and remodeled beginning in 1796.

Even in the early design, Jefferson devised a unique plan for the dependencies. Although there is an early plan detailing the location of a range of rooms semi-detached from the house, by 1771 Jefferson had decided that the dependencies (such as the kitchen, storerooms, service rooms, and quarters for house servants) could be executed in wings partially below ground on the two sides of the mansion, and attached to it with a tunnel or all-weather passage. These wings, however, were not constructed until early in the nineteenth century.

Gardening was Jefferson's lifelong passion, and concurrent with his house building he created orchards, vineyards, and flower and vegetable gardens. Inspired by eighteenth-century theories of landscape gardening, he planned to embellish his grounds with a number of decorative buildings of his own design as well. His 700-foot-long vegetable garden on the south slope of the mountain became his experimental laboratory where he tested an abundant variety of plants.

Jefferson's original grand scheme for Monticello was temporarily cut short in 1782 when his wife died. Soon after her death he left his farms in the care of a neighbor, and returned to public service, which led him away from Virginia for the next eleven years. As minister to France, Jefferson lived for five years in Paris and traveled throughout Europe making notes on architecture and landscape design that he would use as guides for another phase of his Monticello development when he returned.

Beginning in 1794, Jefferson—now a gentleman farmer and out of office—approached Monticello with new energy by restoring his depleted farmlands to create new sources of income and improving the lot of his slave laborers. After studying the latest agricultural practices, Jefferson devoted the first two years of his early retirement from public service to becoming an active farmer, testing new crops, methods, and machines. His most important reform was the substitution of wheat for tobacco as a staple crop and he adopted a scheme of crop rotation and constructed a grist mill to process grain. Jefferson had long wished to abandon the growing of tobacco, a culture he thought "productive of infinite wretchedness," as it impoverished the soil and required constant labor. He reorganized his work force to draw from all parts of the plantation during harvest; the ordinary farming activities at each of the quarter farms were carried out by teams of eight slaves (four men and four women usually referred to as "gangs"), with an overseer at each farm to supervise the laborers.

Like other plantation owners of the time, Jefferson had dreams of economic self-sufficiency, and it was toward that end that he began developing the complex of utilitarian buildings, craft shops, and laborers' quarters between the brow of the south slope of the mountain and a section of the first roundabout road that became known as Mulberry Row. His records show that he had several architectural schemes for Mulberry Row. As early as 1776-78 he envisioned a line of structures that included stone and wooden buildings to house slaves, a greenhouse, and other utilitarian and craft buildings. His first concept included duplexes which were to house slaves in shared apartments. It is clear that some of this early design was brought to fruition, but the 1796 version of Mulberry Row included seventeen structures arranged quite differently from the original plan. Nonetheless, it was along the Mulberry Row that carpenters, joiners, masons, smiths, and spinners and weavers attempted to provide for the needs of the house, the farms, and the more than 125 people living on the estate. Moreover, in 1794 Jefferson attempted to bring in more profit for the estate by establishing a nailmaking shop, supplying the area with that needed commodity off and on for the next two decades.

> I am myself a nailmaker ... I now employ a dozen little boys from 10
> to 16 years of age, overlooking all the details of their business myself
> and drawing from it profit on which I can get along till I can put my
> farms into a course of yielding profit.[1]

It was in this nailery that Jefferson established an incentive system for the slaves: "... them that wukked the best a suit of red or blue; encouraged them mightily. Isaac calls him a mighty good master."[2]

Although a slave holder himself, Jefferson deplored the institution of slavery. After his early efforts failed to introduce a system of emancipation in Virginia, he came to believe that a practical solution to the "abominable crime" of slavery could not be found in his lifetime. He then turned his attention to improving the living conditions of the slaves.

> My opinion has ever been that, until more can be done for them, we
> should endeavor, with those whom fortune has thrown on our hands,

to feed and clothe them well, protect them from ill usage, require such reasonable labor only as is performed by voluntary freemen, and be led by no repugnancies to abdicate them, and our duties to them.[3]

On the other hand, Jefferson suffered from the tension between his humanitarian concerns and the profit from slave labor and multiplication.

My first wish is that the laburers may be well treated, the second that they may enable me to have that treatment continued by making as much as will admit it.[4]

And,

I consider the labor of a breeding woman as no object, and that a child raised every 2. years is of more profit than the crop of the best laboring man. In this, as in all other cases, providence has made our interest and our duties coincide perfectly.[5]

Jefferson freed seven slaves in his lifetime, all members of the Hemings family.

Some of the slave house servants and artisans lived in the various servant's houses along Mulberry Row but when the south wing was completed after 1803, it is likely that many were moved to the wing, leaving some of the wooden dwellings along Mulberry Row vacant. In fact, in 1808 Jefferson specified removing the Mulberry Row structures, but there does not seem to be much written evidence of their demolition during his lifetime. He did, however, direct the construction of a stone dwelling in 1809 to replace a wash house. Perhaps some of the abandoned wooden buildings were pulled down at that time.

Jefferson's years abroad (1784-89) not only affected his attitude about his farm, but they also fostered new design ideas for his house. It was "with a greater eye for convenience" that Jefferson began the long-planned remodeling and enlarging of the house. The final design, inspired by the latest buildings in Paris, was a unique expression of Roman neo-classicism in America. In fact, redesign seems to have been Jefferson's hobby: "Architecture is my delight, and putting up, and pulling down, one of my favorite amusements."[6] Bricks for the remodeling were first laid in 1796, and the house, including the terraces and dependencies planned in the 1770s, was finally completed in 1809. His new plan enlarged the house toward the east, increasing the space from eight to twenty-one rooms (not including the cellars). One of the most striking changes was the addition of the dome, the first of its kind on an American building. Jefferson wanted his four-story house to appear as a one-story edifice, a technique he learned in Paris. The first floor was for rooms of entertainment, bedrooms, and his own study, library, and bedroom, as well as a two-story entrance hall which doubled as a museum. Most other bedrooms and the room beneath the dome could be reached by small private staircases hidden within the spaces over the ground floor one-story rooms.

It is ironic that all during this last rush of building activity Jefferson was living elsewhere. He was engaged in public service, acting both as Vice President of the United States under John Adams, and serving two terms as President from 1801-1809. Because he was usually away from Monticello, Jefferson instructed his workmen through correspondence, which resulted in various records of the construction. Many of these still exist. In fact, Jefferson's passion for record keeping extended far beyond mere building orders and instructions; he also detailed his legal practices, plantation affairs, private finances, and even the daily weather and gardening activities.

While awaiting his permanent return to private life in 1809, Jefferson began creating the major components of his Monticello landscape design. His letters directed an overseer to have slaves construct a 1,000-foot-long terraced area south of Mulberry Row for the laying out of his vegetable garden (fig. 1). He renewed his vineyard and orchard below the garden terrace with plants from Europe and the American frontier. Jefferson also continued to work out his theories of the ideal American landscape in the groves of his mountaintop. From his reading and visits abroad Jefferson developed his new concepts by adapting the principles of the English landscape garden to the climate of the South. He attempted to create a *ferme ornée*, where he laid off the "minor articles of husbandry with ... occasionally the attributes of a garden."[7] His garden continued to be a laboratory where Jefferson tested new plants and cultivation methods in a perpetual search for the hardiest or earliest ripening or tastiest varieties of over 350 plant types.

Thomas Jefferson spent the last seventeen years of his life living at Monticello and retreating to his Bedford County home, Poplar Forest. After his

FIGURE I. *Aerial view of Monticello from the south, 1988.*

death on July 4, 1826, the estate was sold at auction to a Robert Barclay who was said to have plowed the lawns all the way up to the house steps. Retired naval officer Uriah P. Levy bought Monticello in 1836 and used it as an occasional retreat; it was later acquired by his nephew, Jefferson Monroe Levy. The Thomas Jefferson Memorial Foundation, Inc., the current owners and operators of Monticello, acquired the property in 1923.

There is yet another story of the growth and development of Monticello, through the fifty-seven years Jefferson was there and the following century and a half to modern times—that is the story revealed from the buried archaeological evidence. The pages that follow tell of the 1979-1989 archaeological work undertaken to learn about Monticello's landscape design and the plantation community.

CHAPTER ONE NOTES

1   E. M. Betts, ed., *Thomas Jefferson's Garden Book* (Philadelphia: American Philosophical Society, 1944), 235.

2   J. A. Bear, *Jefferson at Monticello* (Charlottesville: University Press of Virginia, 1967), 23.

3   Betts, *Garden Book*, 37-38.

4   Thomas Jefferson to Joel Yancey, 17 January, 1819.

5   E. M. Betts, ed., *Thomas Jefferson's Farm Book* (Charlottesville: University Press of Virginia, 1987), 43.

6   M. B. Smith, *A Winter in Washington, or Memoirs of the Seymour Family* (New York: E. Bliss and E. White, 1824), 221.

7   Betts, *Garden Book*, 360.

Chapter Two

Mountaintop Landscape

Above the ground, historical landscapes have naturally evolved into something quite different from original designs, and modernization obscures signs of the past even more. But below the characteristic manicured lawns that carpet most American historical sites vestiges of the otherwise lost early American landscape can be rediscovered. In conjunction with historical research, archaeologists have been able to recapture a good measure of many aspects of Jefferson's landscape. What one can see is a combination of the practical and idealistic side of Jefferson. For instance, as impressed as Jefferson was with the landscape designs of England (especially the open picturesque parks), he seems to have been realistic enough to know that the oppressive Virginia summer heat necessitated shade. So rather than the open grass and occasional trees of the English park, Jefferson only cleared enough in his grove to create a continuous canopy of branches to provide the desired shade. Or, while Jefferson planned four temples or pavilions along the stone garden wall, it is clear that he decided the common kitchen garden was probably the place for only one of them.

How did Jefferson alter the landscape around Monticello and what were the characteristics of the landscape? Some of the answers have been provided by archaeological research.

The Fencelines

Jefferson enclosed the cultivated area with a fence or paling erected and re-erected over time to divide and secure plants from animals. His description leaves no doubt that his paling made a major statement on the landscape. In 1809, he directed his workman to build:

> … a paling 10. feet high. the posts are to be sufficiently stout, barked but not hewed, 12 f. long, of which 2 f. are to go in the ground. it will take about 300: placing them 9 f. apart.

... The pales are to be of chesnut, riven & strong, 5 f. 3. I long, to be dubbed on one another on the middle rail like clapboards so that I. nail shall do & two lengths of pales will make the whole height. I suppose they will be generally from 5. to 7. I. wide & should be so near as not to let even a young hare in. there will be about 7500. wanting. they are to be sharpened at the upper end thus and not thus as is usual. They are not to be put up till I come home to shew the courses of the inclosure.[1]

Excavations along Mulberry Row revealed the remains of at least four periods of fencelines, two from the Jefferson Period located between and parallel to Mulberry Row and the vegetable garden platform. Patterns of soil discolorations in the ground, evidence of the holes once dug to seat major structural support fenceposts, marked the lines (fig. 2). Remains also included clusters of "shimstones" originally packed around each post and/or organic soil formed by the ultimate decay of the posts (postmolds), and the below ground survival of the post wood or the soil that backfilled the postmold when the post was removed. In plan, the periods of fence postholes form distinct and slightly different alignments that, in turn, establish which postholes belong to which period and, in the case of three of the lines, their relative chronology. The earliest fenceline chronologically, almost certainly erected soon after it was described "to be soon erected" on a Monticello insurance declaration of 1796, was characterized by postholes that were an average of ten feet apart with post shimstones, extending continuously along the brow of the slope of the garden from the

FIGURE 2. *Excavation of garden fenceline postholes, December 1979. View facing southwest toward joinery.*

corner of the joinery ruins almost to the "weaver's cottage," except for a twenty-three-inch gap at the east end of the nailery addition, and where it was evidently attached to various buildings along Mulberry Row (i.e., the storehouse and the smokehouse/dairy). Similar construction and spacing suggest that the 1796 fence also once extended from the southwest corner of the joinery ruins to the nearby carpenter's shop, then to the southwest for 155 feet to a corner, and from there to a terminus 350 feet southeast. Occasional artifacts (such as fragments of annular creamware) found in the soil deposited when the posts were put in suggest a post-1795 construction date for this line. Significantly, other fenceline postholes intruded into the fill in the 1796 fence postholes suggesting that it was the earliest of the fences along the slope.

The next fenceline to stand along Mulberry Row, probably the fence directed by Jefferson in 1808 to be constructed when he came home in 1809, was characterized by large round and relatively deep postholes (averaging two feet nine inches) spaced on an average of nine feet six inches. Often the 1809 fence postholes still contained sections of unhewn (naturally round) locust posts except for the area along the line where a smith's shop and a stone house stood. In fact, the non-survival of wood and an unusually regular spacing along the wall of the smith's shop suggest that these postholes, although they align with the 1809 fence are, in fact, of an earlier period. They appear to mark the location of the building's support posts (of a less durable wood) instead of a fenceline. By the same reasoning, the survival of wood in the postholes along the nailery addition to the smith's shop suggests that these postholes were indeed part of the 1809 fence, pre-dating the construction of that building. If that were the case, it follows that the section of the 1809 fence that runs along the nailery addition wall line later served as the southwestern wall of that structure.

Further toward the northeast it appears that where a smokehouse/dairy stood, the 1809 fence passed through the area encompassed by the building foundation, the post holes penetrating an earth floor or sub-floor proving that the fence post-dated the building. The line was repaired at one point as indicated by another line of postholes and postmolds on the same course. The archaeological evidence of the fencelines was almost at the surface near the joinery and because of that and the survival of wood, the first few 1809 fence postholes appeared to be recent. However, artifacts dating no later than the first quarter of the nineteenth century (transfer-printed pearlware) were the latest datable artifacts found in the 1809 fence deposits suggesting a post-1800 to 1825 date for construction. The latest datable artifacts in the repair postholes (transfer-printed pearlware) also date the probable repair to after ca. 1800. Both the fact of the need for a repair and the survival of so much wood seems to indicate that the fence stood for a long time until it finally rotted away. The "long time" could easily have been more than several decades since locust wood is extremely durable. In fact, it has been demonstrated that in some cases black locust does not begin to decay even after standing for eighteen years.[2]

Instrumental to interpreting the archaeological evidence is Jefferson's 1808 directive to his workman (see above) which lists five construction specifications that could leave archaeological evidence: (1) the length of the new fence—2,700 feet; (2) the time of construction—after 1808; (3) the post material—unhewn locust; (4) the depth of the postholes—two feet six inches, and (5) the spacing between posts—nine feet. Beyond the directive and the plat of 1809, two other references strongly suggest that the paling was built. First is Jefferson's letter of December 19, 1808, to his overseer Edmund Bacon, wherein he states that the garden "… will be inclosed in March …" and, second, on February 24 Jefferson noted that a garden survey line passed "… thro' the covered way of the house and the garden gate … ." Combining history and archaeology, it is logical to conclude that the earliest fence is indeed the post-1796 construction specified on the insurance plat—it is the right date, relatively and chronologically, and it "… connects to or passes very near …" outbuilding remains as the text directs on the 1796 plat. And the later fence and its repair are almost certainly the remains of the line specified in the Watkins directive and shown on an 1809 plat. It has to be at least part of the fence existing in 1809 as only one line was found along the northeastern section of Mulberry Row and the posts are at least the specified two feet six inches in the ground. It is also significant that if one considers that the length of the 1809 plat fence from the Mulberry Row joinery to the southwest corner of the garden (600 feet) is actually a reused section of the 1796 fence, and not "new" construction as the archaeology suggests, then it seems beyond chance that subtracting 600 feet from the full length of the 1809 plat fence shown, 3,300 feet, equals exactly the length of new construction specified by Jefferson to Watkins in 1808 (300 posts nine feet apart, totaling 2,700 feet).

Once the chronology was sorted out, the next goal was to locate points where the interval between posts narrowed from the usual nine- to ten-foot spacing; this would provide clues to gate locations. None could be found in the 1809 line. However, at a point immediately to the south of the all-weather passageway from the house, two larger postholes were found, apparently a gateway. A reference to *the* garden gate seemed to confirm that one and only one gate existed.[3] In all, the excavation traced over 1,000 feet of the likely 1809 fenceline.

Other Garden Features

Excavation uncovered two other key elements of the garden plan: the 1,000-foot-long stone retaining wall along the brow of the orchard slope, and the foundations of a building thought to be the remains of the "temple at the center of the long walk"[4] (fig. 3). (Figure 4 shows the garden wall and pavilion *after* reconstruction.) The stone wall had acted as a barrier to hold the soil removed from the original slope as the leveled platform was created. Because the original slope was uneven, the wall varied in height to retain the garden platform fill. In some places it stood eleven feet high. At the higher points, the wall had to be constructed in tiers. That original stepped construction was not immediately perceptible from the archaeological evidence because so much of the stone had been removed in the late nineteenth century. It was not until the entire span of the 1,000-foot-long wall ruins could be studied at once that the patterns in the rubble became apparent. Such a viewing was possible only through photographs; overlapping stereo photos were taken of the wall from a consistent distance overhead. After gaining that perspective, it is clear that whenever the original stone mason had to build above chest high to exceed the height of his lift, he had to create a platform or tier to stand on.

A stone and brick foundation uncovered at the east-west center point of the stone garden wall left little doubt that a square brick building once crowned one

FIGURE 3. *Remains of garden wall and pavilion foundation during excavation.*

FIGURE 4. *Reconstructed garden retaining wall and pavilion, 1984.*

of the wall's highest points. Specifications in Jefferson's hand from 1811 describe a brick pavilion with a pyramidal roof and a Chinese railing to be built at the center of the "long walk" in the garden. Excavation uncovered brick rubble and mortar below the foundation, apparently debris scattered there by a storm that destroyed the building in the 1820s.[5] The archaeological evidence and the precise Jefferson specifications for the pavilion guided reconstruction of the building.

The Gardens

Jefferson's interest in experimental vegetable gardening was probably exceeded only by his interest in fruit trees. Thus, locating tree planting patterns and terracing in the orchard area where over 150 varieties of fruit trees were planted during Jefferson's time was another major goal of the archaeological research. Assuming that tree growth and leveling of the slope would leave archaeologically detectable marks in the ground, the area southeast of the garden wall was tested before more thorough excavations were conducted. The first tests were conducted with a backhoe digging transects on a northwest-southeast axis along the archaeological grid lines in the hope that soil layers in profile might indicate buried terraces no longer visible at the surface. What appeared to be evidence of slight terraces on aerial photographs on the southeast slope were also cross trenched. While no substantial evidence of terracing showed on the southeastern slope, the southwest trenches did show an undulated surface rising and falling six inches in elevation about every eight feet. Nineteen of these low terraces were found between the garden retaining wall and the present entrance road—the exact number but on a different scale from the terraces described in the vineyard by Jefferson in 1807. And the southwest terrace trenches were not total failures. While no terraces were detected, one cross trench happened to intersect a pattern of dark circular soil stains in the subsoil, exactly twenty-five feet apart northwest-southeast.

Jefferson's planting scheme for the orchard in 1778 and 1811 shows trees twenty-five feet apart in the orchard in that same direction. Another continuous trench was dug at an exact right angle to the northwest-southeast line which turned up stains spaced forty feet apart. Some of the stains were then excavated and found to contain a dark organic soil four inches deep below the subsoil level, the upper eight inches to one foot of topsoil representing a plowzone post-dating the orchard. Over fifty-six of these marks were found, the stains ranging from slight brown marks six inches or less in diameter to rectangular stains three feet by four feet. After the initial two right angle trenches were excavated, the remaining pattern was defined by measuring off a twenty-five-foot distance northwest-southeast and a forty-foot distance northeast-southwest, then removing the topsoil with a backhoe (usually in a three-foot by six-foot trench). As the digging progressed to the northeast, approaching the more severe slope, the soil stains disappeared. However, excavation on the southwest slope, over 600 feet away, uncovered more stains on the forty-foot by twenty-five-foot pattern found to align with the stain lines to the southwest. This suggests that erosion on the steeper slopes in between may have erased the tree stains or that the depth of planting holes could have varied in different sections of the garden. In fact, early nineteenth-century directions for planting orchards recommend shallow holes in certain types of soil, particularly clay.[6] No artifacts except for occasional wrought nails were found in all the planting holes, but seen in light of the existing orchard plans there is little doubt that the planting sequence found is from the Jeffersonian period. The fact that the northernmost two rows of soil stains contain the exact number of tree locations as shown in 1811 is strong evidence for the tree stain pattern.

The Road System and the Ha-Ha

Jefferson's road system held the landscape design together. Before archaeological research, some of the road traces were still visible and in service but other parts had disappeared from view. The roads became the focus of research efforts following the garden study and, like the wall ruins, the archaeological excavation of the road beds actually became the initial grading required by reconstruction. Plats and maps indicated as precisely as such documents can the course of the first roundabout before any digging began. Removal of a parking lot revealed a stone paving and curb and what appeared to be a survey stone marked with a deep chisel cut and an "X" (fig. 5). Locating and recognizing the marker was instrumental in

FIGURE 5. *Stone found along northwestern line of Mulberry Row perfectly level and marked with an "X," probably one of Jefferson's original survey markers for the first Roundabout.*

tying Jefferson surveys to the modern landscape (resurveys of the roadways consistently "closed" within six inches of the marked stone).

The survey stone was the key to determining the course of the road but one of the most convincing archaeological features that indirectly defined the first roundabout was the backfilled ha-ha ditch paralleling the roadway west of the house. The ditch maintained a consistent elevation (like the road), about sixteen feet (or about one surveyors' chain length) from the road. The ha-ha barrier traced a 500-yard course from the South Pavilion south to a right angle turn at the roundabout to end below the modern-day north office. Consequently, the discovery and relatively good visibility of the ha-ha made it possible to trace the western half of the first roundabout. The ha-ha was described in 1823 as a ditch with earth piled on each side and covered with wooden rails as if a fence had fallen across it, a description not unlike that of a modern cattle guard.[7]

Excavations along the north side of Mulberry Row also proved that the yard south of the dependency wing kitchen was once literally paved with domestic trash and garbage, at least from the 1770s until the late nineteenth century. There was obviously no attempt to formally landscape this area; it was a work yard and therefore represented the practical side of the ornamental farm. Excavation in the kitchen yard between the South Pavilion and the vegetable garden platform revealed more of Jefferson's Mulberry Row design and unexpectedly, signs of an earlier scheme. The course of the southern end of the ha-ha and the foundation of what appeared to be a related building were uncovered there (figs. 6a and 6b). But beneath all that, an earlier leveled yard layer and the backfilled cellar of another outbuilding were found, both indicating that Jefferson carried out an earlier landscape plan only hinted at in some of his records and drawings. Both the cellar

FIGURE 6. *(above) House, south pavilion, and kitchen yard excavation, view facing northeast; (below) overhead view of south kitchen yard showing (1) ditch and original kitchen yard leveled area, (2) building A, and (3) dry well during early excavation.*

and the ha-ha house do not appear on either the 1796 insurance plat or the 1809 plat and therefore are not contemporary with either document. But as early as February 1770-71, Jefferson drew a sketch, and later a finished plan, showing a scheme for locating his supporting outbuildings in a line of rooms within a 100-foot long structure located some fifty-two feet southeast of the South Pavilion. The drawing also clearly shows Jefferson's early idea to attach the kitchen, then in the basement of the South Pavilion, to the other dependencies with a weather-protective covered walkway.

The Dry Well

The above mentioned drawing also shows a dry well (or deep cold storage cellar) at the northeast end of the dependencies and stairs into the twenty-three-foot deep cellar.[8] Since no above-ground remnants of this early outbuilding scheme were visible in recent times, and since the 1796 insurance and 1809 plats showed the Monticello outbuildings elsewhere, it seemed unlikely that the plan for the outbuilding rooms in the south kitchen yard was ever executed. However, Jefferson wrote in December 1770:

> ... in digging my dry well, at the depth of 14 f. I observed one digger, one filler, one drawer at the windlace with a basket at each end of his rope very accurately gave one another full emploiment, but note it was yellow rotten stone with a great many hard stones as large as a man's head and some larger, or else the digger would have had time to spare. They dug and drew out 8. cubical yds in a day.[9]

On the other hand, a notation dated 2 August 1771 (apparently added to the 1770 outbuilding sketch) lists specifications for the outbuildings written in the future tense which suggests that little if anything of the brick structure covering the dry well was built. But archaeological excavations proved that the work had been started. Precisely in the location labeled dry well in the 1770 plans, a nineteen-foot-deep backfilled hole was found, almost certainly the excavation described in 1770 that was intended for construction of the dry well. Northwest of that, digging revealed a backfilled ditch (possibly the eroded ha-ha) running north/south toward the center of the South Pavilion on a slight angle to being perpendicular with the course of Mulberry Row. As the ditch fill was removed, the associated soil levels began to show that the area to the southeast of the South Pavilion had originally been leveled far below the present ground surface, deep enough to be level with the first story of the South Pavilion. A three- to four-inch thick layer of dark organic soil containing wood ash and artifacts (dating no later than the early 1770s) was found at a depth of three feet near the pavilion and one foot eight inches at the edge of the dry well. It appears that this surface once formed a leveled eighteenth-century yard, evidently placing the dry well surface and the kitchen floor/doorway on an even plane.

The boundaries of an area projecting beyond the main level of the east and west house lawn precisely where the South Pavilion area was excavated appears on Jefferson's study for the general layout of Monticello in 1770.[10] It seems likely that this projection was to be created for the eventual construction of the 100-foot-long outbuilding and covered-way complex mentioned above.[11] But it seems probable that scheme never went beyond the earth moving stages. Although the dry well construction hole was found in the precise location called for in the plans, and although the kitchen yard once had a lower surface level with the first floor of the South Pavilion kitchen, no archaeological or historical evidence could be found for any masonry or timber construction associated with either the early dry well or kitchen yard. It is clear then that Jefferson changed his plans for the dependencies between August 2, 1771 (the time when he made his notations on the kitchen yard outbuilding sketch) and August 4, 1772 (the date by which he had envisioned the L-shaped dependency wings that were eventually built connected to the house).[12] What caused Jefferson to change his mind during that year is not known, but the change seems to have resulted in the backfilling of the unlined and uncovered deep dry well shaft soon after it was first dug. Why the dry well was abandoned after expending all the effort to dig the initial hole, and whether or not another dry well was dug elsewhere in the south dependencies[13] awaits future research.

Excavations of the dry well showed that the shaft contained eight layers of fill initially resting on a leveled clay floor, all of which appeared to have been deposited first as the results of erosion then as fill dirt to backfill the hole (fig. 7).

Much of the soil was a decomposed greenstone, perhaps the redeposited "yellow rotten stone" referred to by Jefferson where he observed the original dry well excavation in 1770. Large greenstone rocks were also found. In fact, the fill profile shows lenses of "piled" material which could only be the result of intentional back-filling. Thus it appears that soon after erosion became a problem, intentional back-filling began. The erosion and early backfill layers were also separated by an irregular layer of ash sloping in from the northwest. This contained a concentration of domestic artifacts and apparently came from the nearby kitchen pavilion. Above the decomposed greenstone fill two layers of orange clay, also containing greenstone and also separated by another lens of kitchen refuse, were found. These layers appeared to be intentional backfill material as well, generated from the spoil from the original construction excavation and refuse carried from the kitchen. Thus it is almost certain that after some period of erosion, the dirt pile created by Jefferson's diggers went right back into the hole. Following that, apparently the backfill material settled as much as one foot, only to be leveled again by more ash-laden deposits from the kitchen or another nearby building.

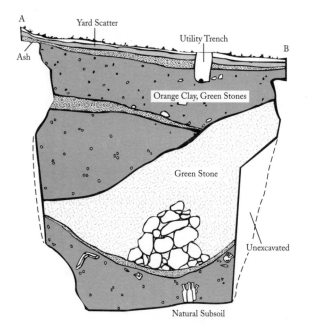

FIGURE 7. *Cross section drawing through layers of backfill in the dry well.*

Both the nature of the artifacts from the fill and their dates suggest a rather quick lifespan for the dry well. English creamware plates, bowls, mugs, and cups were recovered from the fill—all ceramics post-dating ca. 1769. The restorable bottles recovered are all styles dating from the period 1760-90. No artifacts date later than 1771, the year of backfilling suggested by the historical record. Additionally, several fragments of ceramic vessels were found to mend together. This

FIGURE 8. *(left) Group of six bottles found in situ on the dry well floor containing cherries and cranberries.*

FIGURE 9. *(a) Sample of cranberry or crab apple. (b) cherry from dry well bottle.*

suggests they were thrown away at about the same time and that the cellar was backfilled all at one time.

In spite of the fact that the dry well never got its superstructure and probably only lasted a few months in 1771, it nonetheless was used at least once for its intended purpose, as a cooler for perishable food. Six wine bottles of the 1770-1790 style placed on the floor in two rows were found buried by the initial eroded fill. Five of the bottles survived intact, two with corks in place and five out of six with their original contents (fig. 8).

Four of the bottles contained cherries in various states of preservation, ranging in number from 175 to 232 but the fifth contained at least 173 fruits of another kind, possibly a type of cranberry or crab apple (fig. 9). All of the bottles appear to have been completely filled to the neck with the fruit. Analysis of the liquid found no alcohol. It is therefore probable that the bottles were preserving blanched or cooked fruit in a non-alcoholic state. In a letter dated 7 November 1709, William Byrd of Westover in Charles City County, Virginia, described the practice (at dinner) whereby

> "… we had some cherries which had been scalded in hot water which did not boil and then put in bottles without water in them. They were exceedingly good."[14]

The Monticello bottles were probably placed in the dry well's construction shaft for cooling after which they became the victims of a period of wall erosion.

Then they either became irretrievable or retrieval became too much of a challenge for their value.

While soil layers indicate that part of or the full span of the north-south ditch was an early feature in the yard and may have drained the early leveled area, it continued in use and probably became part of the ha-ha system after the old leveled kitchen yard was raised with redeposited subsoil. Artifact deposits in the lower kitchen yard level and the greenstone clay fill above it date to the 1770s, and the ash-laden nature of the old kitchen yard level and the orange clay and greenstone mixture of the layer above are both exactly the same as the soil types used to fill in the dry well (ca. 1771-72). Therefore, it is logical to conclude that whatever had been excavated of the twenty-four-foot by 100-foot platform in the south kitchen yard (according to the early leveling plan) was backfilled at the same time as the dry well shaft. Since the plan for the location of the dependencies changed, the newly leveled yard became as unnecessary as the freshly dug dry well, with the exception of the ditch which continued to drain the area until it became part of the ha-ha.

Although the yard ditch gradually disappears near Mulberry Row after it skirts the western wall foundation of the undocumented mysterious stone building there, that does not indicate that the ha-ha system vanishes as well. The end of another backfilled section of the ha-ha ditch was found about a carriage-gate's width (a gap of fourteen feet as near the North Pavilion) from the building's west wall, suggesting that the building stood for a space along the line of the ha-ha, effectively keeping the barrier continuous. The undocumented stone building foundation consisted of a concentration of greenstone, sandstone, mortar, and brick, forming a rectangle directly aligned with and the same size as the South Pavilion and a stone building directly south of Mulberry Row. The northeast line of the foundation rested and appeared to cut through layers backfilling the ditch, which suggests that the building was either constructed after the ditch was filled or that that section of the existing ha-ha was replaced with the building. In other words, the ha-ha ditch was no longer necessary there since the walls of the building doubled as the barrier.

No earthen-floor level existed within the confines of the stonework; therefore it is probable that the building had a raised wooden floor. Artifacts recovered from a thin layer of mixed clay resting directly on the subsoil, possibly objects lost through cracks in a wooden floor, date the occupation to the post-English shell-edged pearlware period (approximately 1785). A shallow trench paralleling the northwest wall seems to have served some architectural purpose, perhaps to seat floor supports. Early nineteenth-century log construction seems to describe such a technique when it called for the laying of floor sleepers on or in the ground to support "... cleft logs, hewn smooth on one side and notched a little on the underside to lie level on the sleepers or joists ... ."[15] If it is true that the foundations of log buildings consisted of loosely dry-laid stones below grade in trenches, then perhaps the interior trench was dug to construct an even less substantial footing for the floor joist. Or perhaps the joist lay directly in the trench. The lack of a similar parallel trench along the southwest wall could be explained by the overall drop in the ground elevation in that direction. In fact, the extra thickness of the southwest foundation may prove that point. To support a level floor, the downhill sill of the building would have to be elevated three feet higher, perhaps placed on a ledge in the higher and more substantially built southwest stone wall. Of course, it could be that all three of the walls built on the down slope were thicker because they would have to support increasingly higher and heavier walls. Regardless of the construction details, however, there is no doubt that the conscious effort by the builders to align the ha-ha building with the South Pavilion and the stone house on Mulberry Row shows some concern with symmetry even of an apparent work yard.

Soil layers within the foundation trenches of the building consisted of two basic deposits: (1) a loose stone fill with brick, and (2) mortar above a more compact clay packed around larger stones. These two levels were created by both the construction (lower) and destruction (upper) of the structure. Artifacts recovered from the lower level (i.e., English creamware, handpainted English pearlware, wrought nails, and wine bottle glass) indicate that the building was built after approximately 1785, the date *after* which handpainted pearlware became common in Virginia. The more loosely packed rubble with all the brick and mortar in the foundation contained artifacts of a much later date: transfer-printed pearlware and whiteware postdating ca. 1815 and perhaps as late as 1830. This material was most likely thrown back into a salvage trench after the larger foundation stones were removed when the building was destroyed.

The second kitchen yard, south of the present kitchen in the attached south dependency wing of the house, proved less revealing of the yardscape than anticipated (fig. 10). Excavation there did uncover the stone sub-paving of a substantial walkway or driveway leading from the exit of the all-weather passage down the slope toward the garden gate. Elsewhere, occasional postholes and planting holes suggested yard use and appearance but nothing definite about the designed landscape could be determined by the work. The vernacular landscape was also somewhat elusive except that it was quite clear that all during the nineteenth century great quantities of trash were thrown indiscriminately into that yard, and that the entire area except the driveway was deeply plowed. This was not a formal area intended to be seen as a part of any picturesque vista. Unfortunately the plowing erased stratigraphic evidence necessary to sort out other daily utilitarian uses of the yard over time. Testing in the one undisturbed area, beneath the stone paving, suggested that originally there was a wooden surface in at least one section. Artifacts found during the testing suggested a post ca. 1785 date for the walkway/driveway construction.

The Mulberry Row Landscape

The Mulberry Row area was, of course, the strongest vernacular element of Monticello's landscape. There is no doubt from the descriptions that the buildings there were crudely built but they were apparently "better than most [others in Virginia] but striking a contrast to the palace that stood so near."[16] There can be little doubt that a relatively shabby main street stood there. The excavations also clearly revealed that the buildings were surrounded by yards made up of decades of accumulated garbage and trash. But it should be kept in mind that the completion of the dependency wings of the house must have made many of the Mulberry Row buildings obsolete. In fact, by 1809 some of the log houses on Mulberry Row were abandoned.[17] And, it is possible that a stone house constructed in 1809 to replace a log wash house was part of Jefferson's plan to upgrade

FIGURE 10. *View of excavations in the kitchen yard showing stone base of road leading to Mulberry Row.*

Mulberry Row, getting rid of the wooden houses when he constructed more aesthetic replacements.[18] Indeed the largest of the cabins (building "o") with the richest decomposed soil in the yard, seems to have been empty by about 1800. On the other hand, one of three of the smallest and crudest cabins continued in use to as late as ca. 1820. Thus, to one degree or another, the Mulberry Row slave quarters detracted from any overall formal landscape scheme throughout Jefferson's lifetime.

But of more prominence still must have been the so-called "industrial area" located on the western end of Mulberry Row. Excavations there indicated that the blacksmith's shop and attached nailery addition were mere sheds, supported by posts anchored in the ground with no formal foundations. Post buildings are one of the cheapest forms of construction and can appear crude and impermanent. Records and artifact dates indicated that these buildings stood for a considerable period of time—1793 to probably as late as 1819. (While there is considerable record of nail-making at Monticello, there is some question as to the location of the nail-making building or buildings.) Thus, throughout Jefferson's tenure, it seems safe to conclude that the spartan Mulberry Row buildings and yards made a jarring impact on the Monticello landscape.

While all serious researchers admit that there are always aspects of the landscape of the past that are forever gone and unknowable, archaeological research in concert with historical research at Monticello was able to recapture a good measure of the elements of Jefferson's evolving landscape design. The archaeological perspective offers fresh interpretation of the man as well as the land. One only has to read the preamble to the Declaration of Independence to know how idealistic Thomas Jefferson could be. Yet his dreams did know bounds; his training as a farmer taught him the practicalities of life. Jefferson's pragmatic dreaming is as evident in his Monticello architecture as in his mountaintop landscape design. It is clear that the cut-and-paste design of the house blends the classical ideal with the realities of native materials and the accomplishment of craftsmanship with unskilled labor. So, too, in looking at the landscape elements and scaling them next to the plans and concepts left to us in the records, it is clear that while ever striving for the ideal ornamental farm certain realities of time, labor, the topography, and the economic, political, and social realities of Jefferson's own era forced him to compromise.

When considering Jefferson's vast interests, there is always the temptation to concentrate on the unique. Indeed, Monticello and its landscape offer much that is original. But viewed another way, they conform to many typical rules of the day. Jefferson may have criticized the Georgian architecture of the Virginia of his time, yet the way his culture shaped him made him a man of his place and time. For instance, the eighteenth-century preoccupation with individualized space and architectural embellishment of rooms usually and most often seen by the public was apparently a strong influence on Jefferson's planning of the Monticello house. The same subconscious submission to the way he thought things should be is true in Jefferson's landscape design. There Jefferson was guided, like most of his contemporaries, by a mindset trapped in symmetry even when continually faced with the strong reality that the asymmetrical topography of the irregularly shaped Monticello mountain dictated what was possible. It is easy to conclude that the innovative and asymmetrical *ferme ornée* concept guided his layout of the wandering roundabouts. Yet, when one actually walks the land it soon becomes obvious that for ease of transport roads had to be planned to follow relatively consistent vertical grades which, particularly on the north side of the mountain, strike a very irregular curve. But elsewhere symmetry was obviously the goal. Consider the bounds of the rectangular leveled lawns, the rigorous symmetry of the vegetable garden platform, the straight row of houses on the straight Mulberry Row and grid pattern of trees and vineyard on the south slope. In fact, the garden itself is so typical that wherever leveling made it possible, the beds are laid out on near 100-foot increments, a practice followed almost religiously by eighteenth- and early nineteenth-century Virginia planters.

But perhaps the clearest evidence of the strength of symmetry in the Monticello landscape plan is the archaeological discovery of so many landscape and architectural features located along a line that can be drawn across the mountaintop touching the western end of the dependency wings of the house. Indeed, the North and South Pavilions, a dry well building, another unidentified building foundation, the termination of the ha-ha, a stone house on Mulberry

FIGURE II. *Aerial view of Monticello showing quartered space divisions of the landscape as suggested by Jefferson's documents and archaeological building and wall remains.*

Row, the termination of border beds, a drop in elevation on the garden platform, and the garden pavilion all honor that line. Using that line as it bisects the mountain and another perpendicular to it passing through the center of the house, it is possible that Jefferson quartered the mountain in his mind, for planning purposes (fig. II). If that were true, then the quartered plan included: in the northwest quadrant, the grove; in the southwest quadrant, utility and industrial buildings on Mulberry Row, half the garden platform, the garden pavilion and orchard; in the southeast quadrant, domestic servants' quarters, the food preparation and storage dependency rooms, the other half of the garden and orchard with the vineyard; and in the northeast quadrant, the carriage area and a late-blooming orchard. In fact, recognition of that apparent design led to a closer examination of some original mountaintop plats one of which showed scratched lines (often a way Jefferson had of drafting before inking) that formed the exact quadrants suggested by the archaeology.[19] Although it seems that one of the purposes of the scratched lines was to ease the calculation of acreage, it seems beyond mere chance that the lines match what was suggested by the archaeological features on the landscape. Again the symmetry of four equal parts of a pie-shaped mountain could well have been Jefferson's organizing principle.

Jefferson was also typical of his time in that as much as he was concerned with the picturesque and aesthetic, he still had to tolerate the spartan Mulberry Row cabins and put up with the trash-littered side yards all in full view from the house. Recent archaeology shows a similar pattern existed on other Virginia estates of that period as well.[20] Apparently as long as everyone looked straight ahead on and from the formal fronts of the houses, formal architecture or picturesque pleasure gardens met the eye. What was, in reality, going on to the left and right was apparently so commonplace to people of the time, at least rural people, that what modern eyes consider unsightly was probably largely invisible. Indeed, recognizing such land-use patterns is perhaps the most significant contribution of landscape archaeology. And the years of archaeological excavations along the working and living spaces of Mulberry Row clearly defined what it meant to live within Monticello's landscape.

CHAPTER TWO NOTES

[1] Thomas Jefferson to Mr. Watkins, 27 September 1808.

[2] J. C. Wooley, "The Durability of Fence Posts," *Missouri Agricultural Experiment Station Bulletin* No. 312 (1932): 2-3.

[3] J. A. Bear, *Jefferson at Monticello* (Charlottesville: University Press of Virginia, 1967), 12, 87.

[4] F. D. Nichols, *Thomas Jefferson's Architectural Drawings* (Charlottesville: University Press of Virginia, 1978), N-182.

[5] R. D. Gray, "Letters from Henry D. Gilpin to his Father," *Virginia Magazine of History and Biography*, 76 (Oct. 1968): 467.

[6] R. Marshall, "The Rural Economy of Gloucester and Herefordshire," *The Complete Farmer*, 4th ed. (1973); n.p.

[7] Edmund Bacon to Thomas Jefferson, 24 February 1809; E. M. Betts, ed., *Thomas Jefferson's Garden Book* (Philadelphia: American Philosophical Society, 1944), 523; W. Hooper, "Description of Monticello, 20 September 1823," Thomas Jefferson Memorial Foundation Library.

[8] Nichols, *Jefferson's Architectural Drawings*, N-32, N-59.

[9] Betts, *Garden Book*, 17.

[10] Nichols, *Jefferson's Architectural Drawings*, N-34.

[11] Ibid., N-59.

[12] Ibid., N-56.

[13] Ibid.

[14] A. N. Hume, *Food* (Williamsburg: Colonial Williamsburg Foundation, 1978), 42.

[15] Woods (1969), 347.

[16] M. B. Smith, *The First Forty Years of Washington Society* (New York: C. Scribner's Sons, 1906), 68.

[17] Thomas Jefferson to Edmund Bacon, 27 February 1809.

[18] James Dinsmore to Thomas Jefferson, 24 February 1809.

[19] F. Kimball, *Thomas Jefferson, Architect* (New York: Da Capo Press, 1968, rept.), 34.

[20] W. Kelso, "The Archaeology of Slave Life at Thomas Jefferson's Monticello: A Wolf by the Ears," *Journal of New World Archaeology* 6(4) (1986): 5-20.

Chapter Three

MULBERRY ROW

As Jefferson's Monticello house was first taking shape, he was also developing a line of outbuildings to the south which he came to call Mulberry Row. There he eventually directed the construction, reconstruction, or demolition of a complex of servant's houses, craft shops, and utility outbuildings. In modern times only two of these buildings survive above ground—the so-called stone weavers cottage or workman's house and part of the stone stable. Although no drawings in elevation of the buildings are known, in 1796 Jefferson decided to insure his house and some of the outbuildings with the Mutual Assurance Company of Richmond, which required him to map and describe the insured property. This he did in characteristically precise detail. Fortunately the insurance policy survives and is the most exacting documentary "snapshot" of the essentially now vanished Mulberry Row complex. The insurance policy provides a scaled map of each building's location and also lists the dimensions, materials from which they were built, and use. It provides a glimpse at one instant in time in what was an ever-changing yardscape, and it served as an excellent guide for five seasons of archaeological work. This research resulted in the discovery of the postholes, cellars, wall foundations, and artifacts associated with Mulberry Row bringing to light the footprint of Monticello's laboring community.

Some of the 1796 building sites (namely the joinery, nailery, storehouse for iron, and the smokehouse/dairy), were more or less superficially excavated in 1957 and 1958. No excavations were conducted on Mulberry Row for the next twenty years, until an ongoing archaeological research investigation of Mulberry Row began in 1979. This research initially focused on defining a vanished fenceline that documents indicated existed between or among the buildings and the garden terrace below. An archaeological trench several hundred feet long traced the course of the fence line—fencepost hole by fencepost hole. In the process, the Mulberry Row building remains along the line began to be uncovered as well.

Slave Quarters

On the 1796 insurance map Jefferson labeled the largest wooden slave quarter building "o," and it became the first slave house site to be uncovered (see figs. 12-14). He described the building as "a servants house 20½ x 12' of wood with a wooden chimney and earth floor ..."[1] Excavations defined the three foundation walls that survived marked by roughly aligned stones. Near the edge of the road, at what must have been the northwest corner of the building, irregular brick paving contemporary with the house also survived. Excavations inside the line of footing stones uncovered a backfilled stone-lined cellar as well as a small rectangular brick box (small root cellar) centered on the interior of the eastern end of the foundation. A concentration of charcoal in the soil and a scatter of stones just outside the eastern foundation wall line suggested that the wooden chimney mentioned in the insurance description once stood there. Beyond that (to the northeast) another concentration of stone and artifacts defined a trash dumping area and another concentration of the same material indicated a dump to the northwest of the stone footing.

FIGURE 12. *Jefferson's 1796 insurance declaration showing a to-scale line of Mulberry Row buildings with their description, various insured buildings, and the mansion.*

Immediately over the architectural remains a rich deposit of organic soil had built up, in some cases up to three feet deep, at first within the confines of the building foundation and in the cellar. Later in time, the same soil accumulated over the stone foundation itself, across the yard to the east and west and then to the south, apparently against Jefferson's garden fences. This same humic soil filled depressions in the trash areas to the east and west. The occupation layer was so uniform in its appearance, both in color and texture, that except for the deep deposit in the larger cellar and in the two trash areas it could only be excavated as a single deposit.

The datable artifacts from the cabin "o" site established its construction and occupation times from the last third of the eighteenth century to the first decade of the nineteenth century. Handpainted English pearlware, a ceramic type that flooded the American market soon after the end of the

FIGURE 13. *Servant's house "o" and vicinity during early stages of excavation in 1982.*

American Revolution, was the latest datable artifact in the deposit. However, English creamware was the predominant pottery found which suggests that occupation may have begun in the 1770s. The total lack of transfer-printed pearlware from the occupation zone strongly suggests that occupation ceased at about 1810.

FIGURE 14. *Overhead view of the stone foundation, cellars, and brick paving of servant's house "o," Mulberry Row.*

A dwelling should be an excellent indicator of the lifestyle of its inhabitants, but ordinarily it is not possible to come to any precise conclusions about the above-ground appearance of such insubstantially built houses. But given Jefferson's obsession with detailed record-keeping, plus the survival of and opportunity to study a similar contemporary cabin in the Piedmont region, more evidence than usual can be brought to bear on the Monticello Mulberry Row building "o." For example, an architectural and archaeological study made of a slave cabin at nearby Bremo Recess Plantation[2] together suggest a reasonable interpretative reconstruction of building "o" (taken in light of Jeffersonian references to slave quarter construction) despite the lack of any plan or elevation of the building dating back to the Jefferson period (fig. 15).

John Hartwell Cocke, a close friend of Thomas Jefferson, first began building Bremo Recess Plantation in the late 1700s, and it is probable that the one surviving log cabin was used by some of his slaves sometime after about 1825. Because the Mulberry Row buildings were likely built of logs on dry laid stone foot-

FIGURE 15. *Slave cabin at Bremo Recess, Bremo Bluffs, Virginia.*

ings like the Bremo cabin and because the Bremo cabin had a trap door through its plank floor leading to a brick-lined backfilled box near the hearth, the two buildings had enough in common to warrant their comparative study (see fig. 15). The Bremo building is a single pen, V-corner-notched log structure with an exterior stone chimney on one gable end and corner stair leading to a rather spacious attic loft. Immediately in front of the hearth, a trapdoor through the wooden floor leads to a brick-lined box or root cellar (fig. 16). It is clear from the docu-

FIGURE 16. *Hatch cover and brick-lined root cellar in Bremo Recess cabin, filled ca. 1865.*

mentary record that these subfloor compartments were common. Why they were often constructed near the hearth is suggested by Robert Beverly, a Tidewater Virginia planter who wrote in 1705:

> The way of propagating Potatoes … is to bury'em under Ground, near the Fire-Hearth, all the Winter, until the Time comes, that their Seedings are to be set.[3]

If this building were to be destroyed, it would leave essentially the same basic archaeological footprint as building "o" at Monticello, except the more permanent stone chimney would leave a solid foundation and the Bremo building is somewhat larger.

The stairway leading to the loft at Bremo is located in the corner of the room ascending along the gable end of the building opposite the chimney. The brick paving on the northwest corner of Monticello's building "o" suggests that a doorway stood there. But in light of the Bremo plan, it is possible that the Monticello paving served as a footing for a corner stairway. Also, like Monticello's building "o" the Bremo cellar contained rich organic fill and artifacts of domestic life—ceramic and glass fragments, butchered animal bone, and a number of buttons including a gilded military button of a Louisiana Civil War unit.

Although Jefferson describes building "o" as made only of wood, it is almost certain the house was a well-built log cabin. In 1793 Jefferson instructed his son-in-law, Thomas Mann Randolph:

> as I destined the stone house [insurance map building "E"] for work-men, the present inhabitants must remove into the two nearest of the new log-houses which were intended for them, Kritty [a slave] taking the nearest of the whole, as oftenest wanted about the house.[4]

This of course establishes that there were "old" log houses already there and it is likely, judging from the occupation dates of the artifacts, that servant's house "o" was one of the earlier buildings. There were still several log-houses along Mulberry Row as late as 1809 when Jefferson directed his overseer Edmund Bacon to move ex-cook Peter Hemings out of the cook's room in the house dependencies into "any one of the log-houses vacant on Mulberry Row ...."[5] During that same year Margaret Bayard Smith commented on the quality of the slave quarters she passed on Mulberry Row:

> we passed the outhouses of the slaves and workmen. They are all much better than I have seen on any other plantation, but to an eye un-accustomed to such sights they appear poor and their cabins form a most unpleasant contrast with the palace that rises so near them.[6]

Other architectural details are suggested solely by the archaeology. Certain artifacts recovered from the occupation levels tended to concentrate in isolated areas in and around the foundation. Using a computer-enhanced program that maps artifact concentrations, a series of relief maps of the relative numbers of artifacts were made with the data from building "o" (fig. 17).

The study showed a build-up of discarded nails at each end of the foundation, one cluster appearing where the charcoal concentration and the brick root cellar were found. This probably marks the site of the wooden chimney described in 1796. Why the charcoal and nails would form a trail leading away from the site of a wooden chimney is made clear by photos and descriptions of houses of this type recorded in the early twentieth century (fig. 18). Ex-slave interviews and sev-

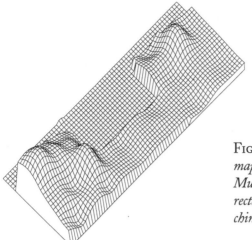

FIGURE 17. *Computer-drawn topographic map of nail concentrations at the ends of Mulberry Row cabin "o" site (recessed rectangle, probably evidence of wooden chimneys).*

eral late nineteenth-century photos show that these chimneys were so easily destroyed by fire that they were often built to lean away from the house partially supported by wooden poles or props. When the stack eventually caught fire, removal of the props and a push would throw the flaming stack away from the cabin, allowing it to survive. A series of these fires would produce a concentration of nails where the chimneys fell. Indeed, to test that theory off site, an experimental wooden frame stack was constructed leaning as far away as possible from a reconstructed log cabin. When the stack was ignited, little effort was needed to send the flaming stack away from the cabin wall, saving the building from the flames

(fig. 19). The stack landed in a heap as the archaeological evidence suggested and burned at a reasonably safe distance from the cabin.

The remains of the five and possibly six other Jefferson period slave houses, three identified on Jefferson's insurance map as buildings "r," "s," and "t," were also the focus of the Monticello excavations (fig. 20).

FIGURE 18. *Nineteenth-century Virginia cabin.*

57

FIGURE 19. *(left) Experimental wooden chimney (above) fire.*

The insurance plat of 1796 describes buildings "r," "s," and "t" in such detail that it is clear that they represent the smallest and probably crudest of the lot.

> r which as well as s and t are servants houses of wood with wooden chimnies, & earth floors 12. by 14. feet each.[7]

Archaeologically the sites of the buildings were in a varied state of preservation: "r" completely graded away, "s" the most intact, and "t" virtually gone with only the bottommost fill of a small root cellar surviving. Nonetheless, since the insurance plat indicates that the three buildings were identical what remained of building "s" can probably serve to show what the plans were for the other two—namely one-room structures with an exterior timber and clay chimney centered on the south wall and with a subterranean root cellar inside near the hearth.

Like the evidence for building "o," it is almost certain that "r," "s," and "t" were made of logs. In 1792, Jefferson instructed his overseer Clarkson to build according to a design of Thomas Mann Randolph:

> five log houses ... at the places I have marked out of chestnut logs, hewed on two sides and split with the saw and dovetailed ... to be covered and lofted with slabs from Mr. Hendersons. Racks and mangers in three of them for stables.[8] (see fig. 21)

FIGURE 20. *Site of Mulberry Row buildings "r" and "s" during excavation.*

A few months after Jefferson directed Clarkson to build these houses, he wrote down a list of specifications for building timber probably to be part of Clarkson's cabins.[9] It is significant that framing "studs" were not included in the order. That indirectly suggests that the "sleepers," "joists," "rafters," and "sheeting" that were ordered were to be used as supports for floors, ceilings, and roofs of several buildings of log construction (i.e., only frame construction requires wall studs; solid log walls do not). It is clear that the 1792-93 log houses were located on Mulberry Row from Jefferson's instruction that Randolph move the slaves from the workman's house (insurance map building "E") to "the two nearest of the new log-houses which were intended for them."[10] This certainly indicates that the new log-houses were located along Mulberry Row and near the workman's house (insurance building "E"), the building nearest the "r," "s," and "t" site.

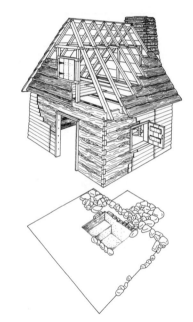

The excavations in that area also uncovered four additional small root cellars filled with domestic refuse indicating that an earlier dwelling stood on the site before building "t" and probably "r" and

FIGURE 21. *Artist's reconstruction of building "s" based on historical records and archaeological evidence.*

"s". And although no foundations were found suggesting the four root-cellar building plan, a Jefferson plan of 1776-78 showing the design for Mulberry Row outbuildings depicts a 17-foot by 34-foot two-room "negro quarter" with a chimney centered on the south wall in the same exact location as the four cellars (see fig. 18a).[11] It is also likely that the building was a multi-family duplex. Jefferson's design indicates that structures with that floor plan were to accommodate "Great George & family, Bradley & Jenny, Betty Hem., Mary, Doll, Betty."[12] Multi-family occupation of larger buildings may well have been Jefferson's original approach to slave housing.

One of the latest house remains discovered (post ca. 1820), a foundation of six brick piers also found in the building "r," "s," and "t" area, seems to represent still another approach to slave quarter design. The brick piers were found spaced evenly about a dry-laid stone footing which either served as a central stove or chimney. The piers indicate that the structure would have had an elevated wood floor suspended well above the ground, thus eliminating the chance for domestic refuse to accumulate beneath the living area as it invariably did in the earlier cabins with dirt floors and root cellars. In fact, pier construction was specifically recommended for health reasons in articles by several planters' agricultural journals published in the first half of the nineteenth century.[13] The space created between the piers allowed free air flow beneath the buildings, effectively eliminating a diseased environment. The pier building survived into the twentieth century and appears in a photograph of ca. 1912 (fig. 22).

Shortly before Jefferson retired from the presidency in 1809, he directed workmen to begin construction of a "stone house" opposite the mansion's south pavilion.[14] Finished in 1809, the superstructure had a relatively short lifespan, owing largely to the fact that it was dismantled down to the lower portion of the stone walls to be used for the enclosure for the 1839 burial of the mother of the new owner of the property, Uriah P. Levy. Excavations around the grave revealed details of the earlier stone house including a massive stone fireplace footing (fig.23). The number of domestic artifacts recovered within the structure and in the sur-

FIGURE 22. *View of Mulberry Row ca. 1912 showing standing Mulberry Row building today (foreground) and what appears to be the superstructure of the pier building (background).*

rounding yard suggest that it was used as a dwelling, probably for slaves. There is considerable certainty about the above-ground appearance of the stone house, for Jefferson directed that it have a pyramidal roof and the ruin suggested that there

FIGURE 23. *Excavation of the stone house/Levy graveyard site showing chimney foundation on the right side.*

was a central door on the Mulberry Row side. The near central fireplace suggests that the structure had only one room, and the hipped roof eliminates the possibility of living space in the loft (fig. 24).

On the 1796 insurance plat Jefferson describes building "l" as "a house 16. by 10½ feet of wood, used as a storehouse for nailrod and other iron" and building "m" as "a house 43½f. by 16.f. of wood, the floors of earth, used as a smoke house for meat, and a dairy."[15]

Indeed excavations uncovered foundations at those locations and of those dimensions (fig. 25). However, the discovery of brick-lined root cellars in the dairy end of "m" and within the remains of "l," as well as the large quantity of domestic refuse in soil strata dating to between 1797 and 1809, suggest that slaves periodically lived in both

FIGURE 24. *Artist's reconstruction of 1809 stone house based on an historical description and archaeological remains.*

FIGURE 25. *Foundation of "smokehouse/dairy" (center background) and "storehouse" (foreground) during excavation. Levy tomb foundation and observation deck in background; Mulberry Row is to the left; view is facing northeast.*

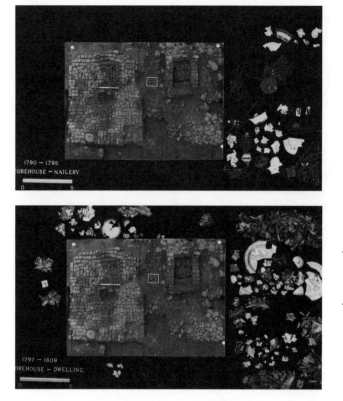

1790 – 1795
OREHOUSE – NAILERY
0   5

1797 – 1809
OREHOUSE – DWELLING
0   5

FIGURE 26. *Overhead view of excavated foundation of the storehouse with: (top) artifacts (primarily nail-rod) found in the deepest occupation level probably from 1790–95 and (bottom) primarily domestic food remains, glass and ceramics from the soil layer above the nailrod deposited ca. 1787–1809. This sequence suggests the building changed from a storehouse for iron to a slave quarter over time.*

buildings, particularly in the so-called "storehouse for iron" (figs. 26). While there is no known record of the above-ground appearance of the smokehouse/dairy or the storehouse, it appears that the dairy had a chimney on one end where ash was found next to a crude brick paving. The building was divided to confine the smokehouse room to a space approximately sixteen-feet square on the west end. That being the case, the living space available for slaves could only be at the dairy end of the structure—an area approximately sixteen feet by twenty-eight feet. The living space in the storehouse, on the other hand, was restricted—two eight-by ten-foot rooms, one floored with brick and the other apparently wood. The root cellar was found in the room without paving, but if the cellar was located near the chimney (in its traditional dry place), then even though nothing survived of its foundation, it is a safe assumption that a fireplace once stood in that room. A distinct scattering of ash in that area and to the west of the wall line may indicate the fireplace as well. It is also safe to assume that the chimney was constructed of wood and the houses of log but there is no direct documentation of house details.

The Lifestyle of Mulberry Row

The excavation of the nine Mulberry Row slave dwellings, buildings "l," "m," the stone house/Levy grave, buildings "o," "r," "s" and "t," the earlier "negro quarter," and the later "pier building," defines certain patterns reflective of the lifestyle of the Monticello slaves. What is probably the most clear from a combination of the historical, architectural, and artifactual evidence is how strongly it seems to indicate social and economic hierarchy within the slave community. Specifically, the research indicated that there was tremendous variation in the quality of housing both at any given point in time and through time (fig. 27). And it seems clear that living standards for slaves improved. A Monticello slave could have lived in something as spartan as a twelve-foot by fourteen-foot log cabin with a dirt floor and a wooden chimney or, on occasion, in something as large and attractive as building "E"—a thirty-four-foot by seventeen-foot stone house with a stone and brick fireplace, wooden floor, and the neo-classical façade Jefferson shows on his design drawing of 1776-78 (fig. 28). While it is true that the excavations showed

FIGURE 27. *Artist's reconstruction of Mulberry Row, ca. 1812.*

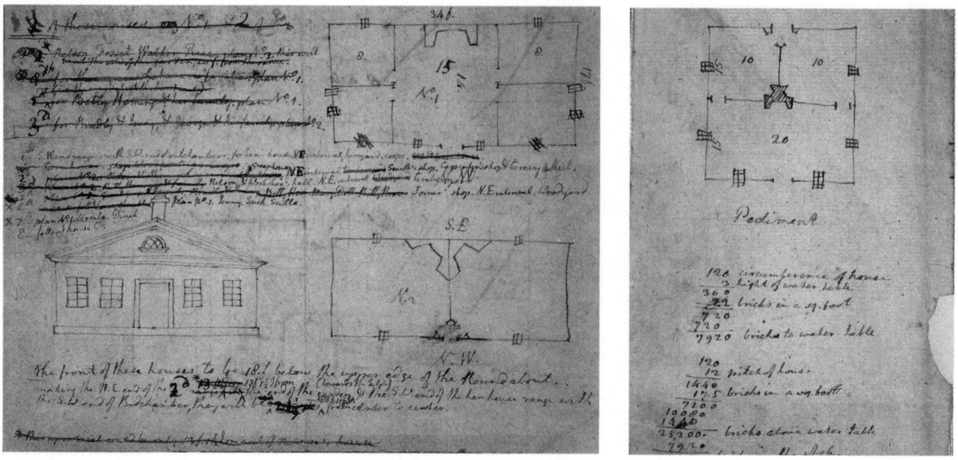

FIGURE 28. *Jefferson's sketch plan of slave quarters for Monticello.*

that such contrasts in housing existed throughout the period, it is fair to say that Jefferson made an effort to replace the cruder log houses, like the tiny building "r," with something as permanent and substantial as the stone house of 1809.

It may come as no surprise that the quality of slave housing could be so varied. Valuable and so visible, it is reasonable to assume that house servants and artisans would have a much higher standard of housing than fieldhands. That may well be true on plantations generally, but documents indicate that only slave house servants, slave artisans, and possibly some mulatto indentured servants and white workmen were given housing on Mulberry Row. Fieldhands lived below the mountaintop on the quarter farms. In that case, the apparent contrasts in the standards of housing reflect a hierarchy within the house servant community itself (i.e., butlers and favored cooks living in the better houses than the maids or laundresses). Or it may be that occupation was not the key factor determining standards of slave housing at all. Perhaps it varied more directly with social status, which in turn was determined in other ways within the white and the black community generally.

There is some reason to believe that during the first two or three decades at Monticello, individuals and slave families were housed in larger barracks-like buildings and were then later relocated into smaller single-family structures. This change seems to have begun during the time when Jefferson returned from Paris (1789) with renewed enthusiasm for improving his farm and the condition of his slaves. It was at that time that he replaced the multi-room "negro quarter" with the matching buildings "r," "s," and "t" and proceeded to move slaves out of house "E." This could represent a change in his thinking about the best way to house slaves. There is no doubt that Jefferson originally intended to house slaves in duplexes or buildings with small apartment rooms judging from a 1776-78 plan (see fig. 27 above).[16] The document shows two seventeen-foot by thirty-four-foot rectangular house floor plans, a two-room and a four-room design, with central doors. On the same sheet Jefferson showed what appears to be the intended elevation for one of the buildings, a surprisingly formal neo-classical façade. His notes show that the four-room plan house was intended for single slaves and the duplexes for two families or single white and/ or black workmen. It appears that only the "negro quarter," the workman's house "E," and perhaps a smith and mason's house were ever actually constructed, and they probably followed the duplex plan.

There is another obvious pattern to the remains of the slave buildings excavated along Mulberry Row. Backfilled root cellars were found in six of them. Ranging in size from as small as two feet by three feet to as large as four feet by six feet, the total of ten cellars found in the Mulberry Row buildings were either unlined or lined with brick, stone, or wood and they all contained very similar artifacts—tools, locks, nails, ceramics, some glass, a considerable number and variety of buttons, and butchered animal bones. Root cellars containing rich organic fill, buttons, animal bones, and metal implements are common to slave quarter sites in Virginia generally. For example, the same types of artifacts were found during the excavation of what was presumed to be the slave quarters at Col. Lewis Burwell's eighteenth-century Kingsmill Plantation and earlier at Carter Burwell's Carter's Grove, both near Williamsburg.[17] During excavations at Kingsmill in 1972-75, building foundations were found encompassing a series of backfilled rectangular pits (at one quarter twenty cellars in all) containing numerous buttons, butchered bone, and usable tools and implements. Indeed, the pattern was so obvious and repetitive during the Kingsmill work, that there could be little doubt from the outset that they would also appear along Mulberry Row at Monticello.

It must be that behavior unique to slaves or at least life for people on the lower end of the social and economic scale accounts for such a predictable cellar pattern. Certainly food storage would be a challenge for people living in the crude dwellings and it is likely that root crops, raised in slave gardens, would be a staple and a necessary supplement for Monticello's usual documented slave ration: one peck of cornmeal, one pound of pickled beef or pork, four salt herring, and a gill of molasses per adult per week.[18] In fact, after their working day and on Sundays, the slaves could turn to improving their circumstances by supplementing these basic provisions from their own vegetable gardens, their poultry yards, by fishing and trapping, and by making clothing and furniture. Slaves also earned money by selling some of these extra staples.

But the fact that the cellars were slowly backfilled over time with similar objects and discarded food remains indicates something beyond mere subsistence. Perhaps these recesses concealed the evidence of pilfering and passive resistance to the labor system. This provides a plausible explanation for the similarities of the contents of the fill. Locks removed from storage rooms would have made pilfering considerably easier, a shortage of tools might make the workday shorter, and leftover bones from the theft of good quality meat could hardly go out in the yard to give the thief away. In fact, there are narratives of masters and slaves alike describing precisely those activities and motives.[19] Colonel Landon Carter of Sabine Hall remarked in 1770:

> This morning we had a complaint about a butter pot being taken from the dairy door where it was put to sweeten last night... Owen had gone over the River... So he could not say whether the servants that lay in house had done it or not. How ever I sent Billy Beale to search all their holes and boxes; And in their loft it was found, but both of them solemnly denying they knew anything of it. I have desired Colo. Brokenbrough to come here within these few days that I may pay those gentlemen for it. It seems such a theft was committed on two butter pots last year but nothing was said about them that I might not be angry; And I do suppose it was expected this would be past over in the same manner.[20]

The holes Carter mentions were undoubtedly the cellars in quarters.

Jefferson knew of the security problems with slaves. So did the slave John Hemings, who wrote Jefferson in 1821 to point out the activities of another slave, Nace, at Jefferson's Bedford County plantation, Poplar Forest:

> I have bin going to Poplar Forest several ... for razing eny kind of vegetable and the very moment your back is turned from thee place Nace takes every thing out of the garden and carries them to his cabin and burys them in the ground.[21]

Jefferson considered the philosophical reasons for the pilfering:

> ... a man's moral sense must be unusually strong, if slavery does not make him a thief. he who is permitted by law to have no property of his own, can with difficulty conceive that property is founded in any-thing but force . . .[22]

Why animal bones, often with the meat still attached, wound up in the cel-lars, might at first seem puzzling, but not if the Monticello slaves acted like ex-slave Charles Grandy:

> I got so hungry I stealed chickens off de roos' Yessum, I did, checkens used roos' onde fense den, right out in de night. We would cook de chicken at night, eat him an' bu'n de feathers. Dat's what dey had dem ole paddyrollers fer. Dey come roun' an' search de qua'ters fer to see what you bin stealin'. We always had a trap in de floor fo' de do' to hide dese chickens in.[23]

The accumulation of all of these things, artifactual and organic, brought on more serious problems. A nineteenth-century Virginia slave owner described what ultimately happened at the older slave houses on his plantation:

> On my own farm a few years ago, typhoid broke out in an old negro cabin, closely underpinned and which for many years had been used as a negro house. My family physician advised me to tear away the underpinning and have all the filth cleaned up. In doing so, I found

an accumulation of foul matter in layers almost denoting the number of years it had been collecting.[24]

The historical record of slave life at Monticello is probably among the most complete of any plantation from the slave era in Virginia. And although there are complete lists of the domestic slaves for the Monticello home farm, there appears to be no sure way to know who lived where. The most prominent slave family was that of Betty Hemings, who Jefferson inherited in 1774 from his father-in-law, John Wayles. Betty was the daughter of a slave woman and an English sea captain and it is likely that John Wayles was the father of five of Betty's children: Robert, James, Peter, John, and Sally. Another prominent resident slave family on the mountaintop was that of Great George and Ursula, and their son, Isaac, who Jefferson sent to Philadelphia to learn the tinsmithing trade. He apparently set up shop thereafter on Mulberry Row, but while he was skilled at his job, the tin shop does not seem to have been enough of a success to stay in business.

On the other hand, using the 1796 list of people who worked and/or lived at the mountaintop part of Monticello, coupled with occasional isolated references to individual shops and buildings, can sometimes hint at who may have worked in a given Mulberry Row location. In any case, the list at least begins to give individual identity to people who are usually lumped together as slaves, even if it cannot always pin down each individual to a specific place. A "bread-list" (as it was called) recorded the amount of cornmeal each worker received each week. Under Monticello Jefferson lists fifty-seven slaves and three white workers (apparently the total population of the labor force in 1796), ranked in ascending order by what appears to be status according to the relative importance Jefferson placed on their occupation and whether or not they were white or the children of the mulatto slave, Betty Hemings.

Mr. Bailey (the head gardener), Mr. Buck (carpenter), and Mr. Watson (carpenter and joiner), all three white, are listed first after "the House," followed by children of Betty, all quadroons (one quarter black) or mulattoes (half black) and all house servants, crafts people, or children. Only John Hemings, the skilled joiner, is listed apart from his relatives for some unknown reason. It seems reasonably clear that Critta lived in the small cabin "r" with Sally or Sally lived in cabin "s" next door. It may not be coincidence that excavations recovered an artifact bearing an inscription that may link the object with either Sally or her brother, James. From a strata of domestic refuse spilling down the slope south of the cabin "s," a French faience apothecary jar (fig. 29) was found with this inscription:

Teiſſier P.f.m Rue
de Richelieu vis a vis
le Café de Foi
Paris

FIGURE 29. *French faience pharmaceutical jar from the apothecary of "P.f.m. Teissier" found on the garden slope below Mulberry Row, building "s."*

The inscription seems to be an advertisement for a certain P.f.m. Teissier whose shop or restaurant/café was located on Richelieu Street directly across the street from the Café of Toussaint Foy, which was located at 46 Rue de Richelieu from 1725-1784. After 1784, the Café de Foy relocated in an arcade in the Palais Royal, where it continued to be a rendezvous of "women of quality." Such establishments suitable for women were rare. In any case, the jar had to have been made no later than 1784, the year Jefferson arrived in Paris as United States minister, or its address would have been obsolete. Jefferson belonged to a chess club located above the relocated Café de Foy, and he frequented the Palais Royal shops, restaurants, and theaters. He also had James Hemings, the cook, with him during his entire stay in Paris (1784-1789), and Sally Hemings (with his daughter) joined them in the summer of 1787. It is possible that the jar, usually a vessel used for ointment or various lotions and drugs, was purchased by either one of the Hemings during their stay there and ultimately the empty jar disposed of behind Sally's cabin.

Sally may have lived in cabin "s" until at least as late as 1809, for the jar was

FIGURE 30. *Daguerreotype of Isaac, tinsmith and blacksmith at Monticello.*

deposited on a slope that was created during the 1809 excavations required for the construction of the garden platform below the cabin. Sally was said by Thomas Jefferson Randolph to have later lived in quarters at the southwest end of the south wing of the house, so the jar may have been discarded before her move to that location.[25]

After Sally and Betty, Jefferson lists his honored and soon to become overseer, George, George's wife Ursula (a trusted house servant), two of their children—the blacksmith/tinsmith (Isaac) (fig. 30) and George (the blacksmith who ran the nailery), and two nail boys (Kit and Philip). Then John Hemings (the joiner), Phill (shoemaker and carpenter), his wife Aggy, Tom (the carter), Goliah (field laborer), and Mingo (perhaps a gardener), and his wife Fanny. Jefferson then listed Jupiter who was at times his personal body servant, coachman, groom, and stablemaster and Jupiter's family, wife Suckey and children Philip, Zachary, and Suckey. Jupiter seems to have had an on-again, off-again friendly relationship with his master. When the house was being remodeled in the 1790s, Jupiter was given the lower status job of blasting and hauling rock and limestone, yet Jefferson expressed deep loss when he died in 1800. The circumstances reveal African-American medical and spiritual tradition. Of his death Martha Randolph wrote:

> [Jupiter] unfortunately conceived himself poisoned and went to consult the negro doctor … He went in the house to see uncle Randolph

who gave him a dram which he drank and seemed to be as well as he had been for some time past, after which he took a dose from his black doctor who pronounced that it would *kill or cure*. 2 1/2 hours after taking the medicine he fell down in a strong convulsion fit which lasted from ten to eleven hours during which time it took 3 stout men to hold him. He languished nine days but was never heard to speak from the first of his being seized to the moment of his death. [The black doctor] absconded.[26]

Other signs of black folk tradition were found along Mulberry Row. It is clear that an African cowry shell, pierced coins, and a finger ring made of horn are ethnic survivals (fig. 31). The shells were used as currency in Africa until the late nineteenth century and adorn spiritual costumes. The ring, made of (cow?)

horn, is likely a *mojo* or magical charm, a type of jewelry still being made in Jamaica. Pierced coins were worn by blacks for jewelry and religious purposes as well. The fact that these spiritual objects represent such an infinitesimal percentage of the Mulberry Row collection is probably misleading. African spiritual practices undoubtedly played a major role in the lives of slaves but would leave relatively little in the archaeological record. That it left any record at all at Monticello underscores its importance among Jefferson's slaves.

FIGURE 31. *Artifacts from Mulberry Row reflecting African roots of Monticello slaves. Top left: Indian Ocean cowry shell; bottom left: horn ring; right: Spanish silver coins drilled for display.*

Following Johnny, the gardener, the rest of the bread list names fourteen slaves hired from other plantations and eight boys who worked in the nailery, apparently completing a thorough listing of the Monticello/Mulberry Row labor population of 1796. These were Jefferson's "people" in that year, and very little seems to change through time. Twenty years later (1815), the bread list names fifty-nine slaves; eighteen are relatives of Betty Hemings and twelve of these are the first to be listed.

How much of the documents, artifacts, and buildings of Mulberry Row reflect the lives of the Hemings family and how much they are reflective of the more heterogeneous laboring community at Monticello is uncertain. That being the case, it would be irresponsible to make many broad generalizations about slave life in Virginia based on what was found on Mulberry Row. How many other households and craft operations on Virginia plantations of the Monticello scale were run primarily by slave mulattoes and quadroons who were in-laws of the master's wife remains to be seen. On the other hand, there is some reason to conclude that many of the Virginia plantation slaves by the end of the eighteenth century were as racially mixed as Monticello:

> In Virginia mongrel negroes are found in greater number than in Carolina and Georgia; and I have even seen, especially at Mr. Jefferson's, slaves, who, neither in point of colour nor features, shewed the least trace of their descent; but their mothers being slaves, they retain of consequence, the same condition. This superior number of people of colour is owing to the superior antiquity of the settlement of Virginia, and to the class of stewards or bailiffs, who are accused of producing this mongrel breed.[27]

It seems clear from documentary sources, and perhaps the houses and the artifacts recovered, that the material world of the Monticello mountaintop slaves had become primarily Anglo-American. That is, what slaves lived in and the objects they used, with a few exceptions, were not in any obvious sense reflective of African heritage. Whether or not the way objects were used was more African or African-American than Anglo-American based on archaeological evidence is extremely difficult to know. For example, whether the presence of a teacup on a slave site means it was used for tea drinking might be questionable. A good deal more must be learned about African culture and the folklives of African-Americans and Americans of African descent before such questions can be answered. But how spartan the standard of living was for slaves compared to others in colonial society is an archaeologically answerable question. Part of that answer comes from another Monticello site—the house site of two free white laborers and their families.[28]

The Stewart-Watkins House

Maps and other records pinpoint where the white Monticello blacksmith (William Stewart) and the carpenter (Elisha Watkins) and their families lived from 1801-10. The house was located some 500 feet from the southwestern end of Mulberry Row.

Stewart was a talented blacksmith from Philadelphia who lived at Monticello with his wife Mary (until she died in 1803) and his three sons, Charles, John, and William and at least two daughters. He was hired to run the nailery, produce the hardware for Jefferson's new Monticello milling operations, and perform general smithing for a salary of $155 per year in cash and 500 pounds of pork and corn. After his wife died, he may have had a slave woman live in the house to conduct the daily domestic chores. He was always praised for his talent but admonished for his drinking and finally dismissed by Jefferson entirely; he left Monticello in 1807.

FIGURE 32. *Overhead view of Stewart-Watkins house site, 1990.*

FIGURE 33. *Farm-house interior suggesting Stewart–Watkins house showing trap door to root cellar (center foreground) and stone with brick base (background).*

The following year Watkins moved in with his wife and two young slave boys. He was employed building the garden paling and roof for the 1808 stone house. Little more is recorded about his Monticello activities and he appears to have left the mountain by 1809. Thus, the site was probably abandoned after Watkins' single year of residency, making it a time capsule of the first decade of the nineteenth century.

Excavations of the Stewart-Watkins site revealed a rather peculiar foundation footprint that included stone foundations and what appear to be stone and brick chimneys at each end of a probable doubled (two pen) log house measuring at least eighteen feet by thirty-six feet at its most developed state (fig. 32). The house also had a sizable wood-lined cellar on the east and a strange brick footing—perhaps a stove base inside and at the mid-point of one wall (fig. 33). It was built into a steep slope, which leaves no doubt that it had a raised wooden floor.

How does the Stewarts' house contrast with the Mulberry Row slave quarters? Both were built of logs, material used by the "poorer sort," yet "cooler in summer and warmer in winter" compared with frame construction. But Stewart had almost three times more ground level floor space than the largest of the Mulberry Row cabins (648 square feet to 240 square feet at building "o"). The Stewart house brick and stone chimneys were also safer and required less repair than the timber clay stacks of Mulberry Row. The raised wooden floor at Stewart's was also drier and more sanitary than the earthen floors of Mulberry Row.

The Shops

While historical records and excavations showed that the living quarters of Jefferson's laborers along Mulberry Row were either built of log on a stone foundation or were built of stone, most of the substantial shops where they worked, located at the western end of the road, were clapboarded buildings with framing seated directly into the ground. Excavation at the sites of buildings "d," "j," and "i" (the blacksmith's shop later expanded by the addition of a nailery building and the carpenters' shop), uncovered earth floor levels and lines of postholes where the main framing timbers of the buildings were seated into the ground. The most substantial of these sheds was the smith's shop where excavations uncovered the lines of postholes for the frames spaced around an uneven paving of stone (fig. 34).

The stone seems to have acted as an aggregate material to firm up an earth floor above it (removed apparently by excavations at that site in 1957) and perhaps for drainage for the floor surface during wet weather. Three circular gap areas in the stone paving suggest locations where wooden stumps to support anvils were located, and a certain regularity in the stone paving along the north wall line seems to pinpoint a doorway location. The 1957 excavation of the smith's shop site removed the earth floor level without precise record of artifact location. It was therefore not possible to locate specific blacksmithing activity within the building. But there is some reason to believe that the drawing Jefferson made of a blacksmith's shop that includes three forges and circular anvil bases and the archaeological remains are the same building; it is the same size and the door openings seem to be identical (fig. 35).

FIGURE 34. *Nailers' addition "j" after excavation. White markers locate anvil holes. Photo facing south.*

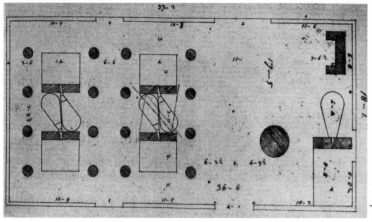

FIGURE 35. *Jefferson's plan for his nailery which was located on Mulberry Row.*

The 1957 excavation work did not remove most of the working floor levels of the nailery addition which had been built onto the east end of the smith's shop (fig. 36). The postholes left from the framing of that structure outlined a dirt floor that was left to accumulate discarded and lost iron waste over a period of what appeared to be the eighteen-year lifespan of the building (approximately 1794-1812). Therefore, the location of the artifacts and their relative distribution inside the wall lines are a clear indication of how the nail-makers and their occasional other black-

FIGURE 36. *View of re-excavation of the smith's shop.*

smithing work was carried out in that part of the smith complex. For example, concentrations of waster nails and clinker on the east end of the building in and around two circles of anvil stump holes gave the clear impression that nails were made there around two table forges. And at the other end of the building, concentrations of charcoal, stones, band or hoop iron, and many partially made machine-cut nails indicate that a nail-making machine and related forges were located in that end of the building (fig. 37). Conversely, the lack of concentration of waster nails toward the center of the building suggests a storage area or perhaps a space reserved for packing nails and other products. And the spacing of the ground seated posts along the north wall in the same area suggests that a ten-foot wide door existed in that area.

The over 1,000 pounds of waster iron recovered from the site is particularly reflective of the quality and quantity of the smithing operation. Besides the primary product, hand wrought nails, chains, tools, guns, carriages, building hardware, and horseshoes were made and/or repaired. Some recovery of ceramics and glass also suggests a certain amount of domestic use

FIGURE 37. *Metal waste and other artifacts in the southeastern corner of the nailery.*

of the building as well. It is possible that the nailers, mostly slave boys, lived in the buildings some of the time. Excavations at the carpenter's shop site revealed little structural remains except for seven postholes where main support posts of the shop had been seated in the ground, two lines of three on the north and south and one at the center of the west wall. It is possible that the single west wall hole is evidence of a door or chimney hood. No earth floor levels survived and as one might predict at a carpenter's shop site, few artifacts except for nails were found. Of particular interest and mystery was the discovery of a number of small iron objects that seem to be small one-half-inch-long nails with points at each end. Since there is some mention that shoemaking was done at the shop at one point during its existence, it is possible that the unusual "nails" were used by cobblers.

CHAPTER THREE NOTES

[1] Thomas Jefferson to Edmund Bacon, 27 February 1809.

[2] W. M. Kelso, "Survey of Bremo Recess Plantation," Manuscript, Thomas Jefferson Memorial Foundation Library, 1983.

[3] R. Beverly, *The History and Present State of Virginia*, ed. L. B. Wright (Chapel Hill: University of North Carolina Press, 1947).

[4] Thomas Jefferson to Thomas Mann Randolph, 19 May 1793.

[5] Thomas Jefferson to Edmund Bacon, 27 February 1809.

[6] M. B. Smith, *The First Forty Years of Washington Society* (New York: C. Scribner's Sons, 1906), 68.

[7] F. Kimball, *Thomas Jefferson, Architect* (New York: Da Capo Press, 1968, rept.).

[8] Thomas Jefferson, "Memorandum for Mr. Clarkson," 23 September 1792.

[9] Thomas Jefferson, "Scantling for the Operations of 1793," Library of Congress.

[10] Thomas Jefferson, Letter to Thomas Mann Randolph, 19 May 1793.

[11] Kimball, *Jefferson, Architect*, No. 56, p. 16.

[12] Ibid., 56.

[13] J. O. Breeden, *Advice Among Masters* (Westport: Greenwood Press, 1980).

[14] Thomas Jefferson, Letter to Edmund Bacon, 17 October 1808.

[15] Kimball, *Jefferson, Architect*, Fig. 136.

[16] Ibid.

[17] W. M. Kelso, "Excavations at Carter's Grove, 1970-1971," Manuscript, Colonial Williamsburg Foundation, 1971; *Kingsmill Plantations, 1619-1800: Archaeology of Country Life in Colonial Virginia* (New York: Academic Press, 1984).

[18] Ration calculated from various sources by Lucia Stanton, Senior Research Historian, Monticello.

[19] Kelso, *Kingsmill Plantations*, 118-128.

[20] J. P. Greene, ed., *The Diary of Colonel Landon Carter of Sabine Hall, 1752-1778*, (Charlottesville: University Press of Virginia, 1965), 495.

[21] John Hemings, Letter to Thomas Jefferson, 29 November 1821.

[22] Thomas Jefferson, Letter to Dr. Edward Bancroft, 26 January 1788.

[23] C. Purdue, et al., *Weevils in the Wheat: Interviews with Virginia Ex-Slaves*, (Charlottesville: University Press of Virginia, 1976), 116.

[24] Breeden, *Advice Among Masters*, 130.

[25] See Henry S. Randall to James Parton, 1 June 1868, in Milton E. Flower, *James Parton: The Father of Modern Biography* (Durham: Duke University Press, 1951), 236.

[26] Martha Jefferson Randolph to Thomas Jefferson, 30 January 1800, in E. M. Betts and J. A. Bear, Jr., eds., *The Family Letters of Thomas Jefferson* (Charlottesville: University Press of Virginia, 1986), 182-183.

[27] Duc de La Rochefoucauld-Liancourt, *Travels Through the United States of America in the Years 1795, 1796 and 1797*, Vol. 3 (London: T. Gillet, 1800).

[28] B. J. Heath, "A Report on the Archaeological Excavations at Monticello, Charlottesville, VA, The Stewart/Watkins House, 1989-1991" (1991). Manuscript on file, Department of Archaeology, Monticello.

Chapter Four

THINGS OF EVERYDAY LIFE

Clearly the Monticello archaeological evidence could best be understood if there was a way to determine who used each of the thousands of objects recovered. But the nature of archaeological remains, as with most circumstantial evidence, usually makes that level of precision impossible. Still Jefferson's dedication to meticulously recording life at Monticello occasionally makes it possible to pinpoint certain things to time-capsule-like instants, to associate some objects with small groups within the Monticello community and though rarely, to tie some things directly to individuals. Certain documentary references and the location of where certain artifact deposits were found makes possible the division of the collection into four categories: (1) objects likely to have belonged to Jefferson and his

family and used in the house, (2) objects that were used by slaves in quarters along Mulberry Row, (3) objects that were used by some free white laborers, and (4) objects that were finished products, waste products, or tools of Monticello industry and agriculture.

It seems likely that objects found along the foundations of the mansion or relatively near it were used by Jefferson and his family. By the same token, things found in the cellars, dirt floors, and with some reservation, the surrounding yards of the Mulberry Row servant's houses, probably once belonged to slaves. It is

FIGURE 38. *View of excavated stone drain along foundation of Monticello mansion.*

also clear that artifacts found at the isolated and briefly occupied house of William Stewart and Elisha Watkins were used and discarded by free white laborers and their families, and there is a degree of certainty that iron objects found at the smith's and nailer's shop site represent blacksmith's manufacturing or repair work. It is also logical to assume that many objects were passed around from site to site and from family to labor force or labor force to family.

From the House

Archaeological excavations along the foundation of the house were not included in the original Monticello archaeological project. The thought of digging in this location seemed pointless as installation of the existing modern roof downspout drains had already seriously disturbed Jefferson period soil layers along the house footing. And even if some of the soil layers were intact, it seemed unlikely that any significant artifacts would have wound up along the walls. The side yards of estates like Monticello were the traditional household dumping grounds, not the immediate grounds of the house. It was not until the decision was made to totally rebuild the deteriorating roof of the house and its drainage system that conducting archaeological excavations near the house was considered on the chance that something significant might turn up when construction crews (instead of archaeologists) dug the trenches for new run-off drains. The foundation areas then became the focus for archaeology. Good thing! In the process of redoing the roof and drainage system considerable quantities of ceramics, glass and a number of significant miscellaneous small finds were recovered. And their presence directly next to the house assured that they were representative of the types of things that were once used in the house by the Jefferson family.

Most of the house foundation artifacts were found in an area adjacent to Jefferson's bedroom and study in the fill of a deep unfinished stone drain (fig. 38). There is every reason to believe that these objects began to accumulate there after a new drainage system rendered the partially built stone drain obsolete. The ceramics found in the fill suggest backfilling of the drain slowly over the period ca. 1780-1815. Artifacts along the southeast foundation were likely thrown there after 1794, the date when the house expansion began in that direction.

Generally, the foundation artifacts consisted of relatively small fragments of ceramics and glass or building materials such as broken bricks and nails. The extremely fragmentary nature of the ceramics and glass seems to indicate that they could have wound up along the foundations as the end product of general housekeeping; that is, these deposits were the accumulations of floor sweepings thrown along the footings from the nearest door or open window. The building materials are more easily explained. They represent fallout from construction or alteration to the house. Of particular interest in this collection were two parts of a heavy wrought iron lightning rod grounding system, probably once as vital to protecting the mountaintop house from fire as its modern counterpart.

The foundation artifact collection also contained brass parts and accessories from a microscope (fig. 39). Probably nothing could be more reflective of Jefferson, the ever-inquisitive scientist, than these instrument parts. At first glance it may seem surprising that parts to such valuable and prized possessions would ever get lost, but it is likely that Jefferson's microscopic experiments were done on a window sill where he could catch the sunlight. In that case, the small round objects could have easily rolled off the sill to become lost along the foundations. The bone mouthpiece to a musical instrument (a recorder) was also found along the foundation.

The ceramics from around the foundation consisted of fine quality porcelain

FIGURE 39. *Collection of scientific instrument parts from the mansion foundation. Left to right: microscope "objective," "o" ring for microscope viewing slide, tinted lens.*

in specialized forms such as a Delft bottle, large pitcher, and a porcelain punch bowl. Fragments of Chinese porcelain of lesser quality, including a blue and white type of plate so commonly found on slave quarters along Mulberry Row, were also found there. Fragments of wine glasses and what appears to be a medicine or chemical vial with the letters "Satur"[ate?] scratched onto its shoulder were found in the drain.

There is a good chance that the hundreds of artifacts found in the dry well backfill also were discards from the house—but only the *earliest* house (1770-1794) (see fig. 6b). The fill was eventually thrown into what appeared to be an aborted dry well from the direction of the nearby kitchen (south pavilion, first floor). It is probable that the fill went into the shaft in the winter of 1770-71, as this was the period when Jefferson records slaves digging the cellar hole. It is also about this same

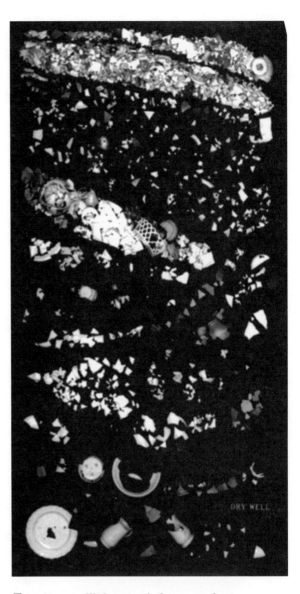

FIGURE 40. *All the ceramic fragments from dry well deposits, top to bottom.*

time that he changed his plan and decided to place the outbuildings in attached subterranean wings closer to the house. Consequently the shaft was probably backfilled in short order even though the wing was not actually completed until 1803. The 1770-71 date of deposit of the dry well is supported by the manufacturing dates of the ceramics and stylistic dates of the cherry bottles as well. Therefore, this is likely a collection of some of the earliest Jefferson family possessions.

FIGURE 41. *Assemblage of ceramics probably used by the Jefferson family in the house. Top, left to right: transfer printed pearlware platter, painted pearlware patty pan, creamware plate, white saltglazed stoneware mug. Bottom, left to right: creamware basket, creamware plate, creamware cup and saucer (?).*

FIGURE 42. *Assemblage of Chinese porcelain plates, a bowl, teabowls, and saucers.*

FIGURE 43. *Collection of ceramics found thrown behind the garden wall during construction in 1808.*

The thousands of fragments of ceramics in the dry well fill represented a minimum of ninety-four different vessels, mostly English Staffordshire creamware or Chinese porcelain with fine handpainted designs over the glaze (figs.40-42). Included with the collection are English white salt-glazed stoneware mugs and a finely executed pierced creamware basket. Of particular interest in the collection was the recovery of a lead glass decanter engraved with grapevines, clusters of grapes, and labeled "madeira"—a wine favored by Jefferson in his younger days.

A deposit of artifacts in builder's fill behind the vegetable garden retaining wall created another chance time capsule near the foundation of the garden pavilion. It is possible to date the deposit near the pavilion to between April and December 1808 because correspondence dating to that period between Jefferson and his overseer, Edmund Bacon, details construction of that particular section of the garden retaining wall.[1] Thirty-six ceramic vessels and some glass vessels were found packed together in fill directly behind an elevated portion of the stones, obviously deposited there during construction (fig. 43).

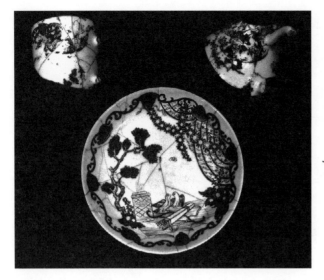

FIGURE 44. *Overglaze decorated polychrome Chinese export porcelain saucer (restored) with matching "pitcher" (right) and cup (left) from the garden wall ceramic deposit. The design is known as the "Altar of Love" or "Valentine" pattern, used on vessels made ca. 1740-60. (Diameter of saucer is 11.7 cm.)*

The cache included fifteen vessels from an overglaze Chinese porcelain matched teaware set bearing a design that included an altar holding a burning heart, love birds, and cupids' arrows (fig. 44). This pattern, known as the *Altar of Love* or *Valentine* pattern, was based on a 1743 English painting by Piercy Brett, which was adopted for Chinese and English porcelain during the middle and third quarter of the eighteenth century. Other high quality tableware was found in the same deposit, including a Delft punch bowl and a blue and white patty pan, all vessels that could have been on the table as part of a dessert course. It is possible that this deposit represents an attempt by a house slave to hide evidence of dropping and breaking a tray full of dinner dishes. This ceramic deposit shows a good sample of Monticello's tableware of the era, and the early dates of some of the ceramics (like the *Altar of Love* porcelain and the Delft punch bowl) suggest that some of the house furnishings were becoming "antiques" for their time.

From the Slave Quarters

Fragments of at least 289 ceramic vessels were recovered at building "o" from the fill of the largest cellar, the earth floor of the house, and in the surrounding yard for a considerable distance east and west (fig. 45a and 45b). The collection includes thirty different forms and thirty-six different types, all primarily tableware and predominantly either English creamware or pearlware and Chinese ex-

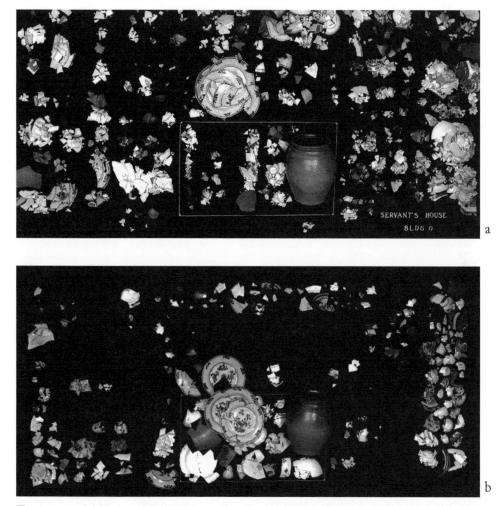

FIGURE 45. *(a) The total ceramic fragments from occupation layers in and around cabin "o" shown here in their relative association with the outline of the cabin foundation (rectangle). (b) The same ceramics arranged according to crossmends between the yard and the house floor.*

port porcelain. The collection also includes fifteen matching underglazed blue Chinese export porcelain plates. From this it would seem logical to conclude that slaves along Mulberry Row had a share of some of the best ceramics available. On the other hand, one could reasonably question whether what is found on the sites of the slaves' houses so close to the mansion was discarded there as mansion trash, having nothing whatsoever to do with the lifestyle of the black labor force. But exactly where on the cabin site the vessels were found helps sort that out. For example, some fragments of yard vessels are found imbedded in the dirt floor levels of cabin "o." From this evidence one could be reasonably sure that the dirt floor vessels were used and broken by slaves in that house and the rest of the shattered pieces thrown out into the yard. That this was so is illustrated by Figures 45a and 45b. They show two overhead views of all the ceramics found at building "o." Figure 45a shows the ceramics laid out according to whether they were found *in* the house floor (therefore placed *inside* the rectangle) or in the surrounding yard. The same ceramics laid out according to whether or not yard fragments mend onto or otherwise match fragments found in the cabin dirt floor are shown in Figure 45b. From this it is clear what and how much of the yard material seems to have been used and broken within the cabin and presumably how much of the collection may have been trash from the mansion.

In fact, most of the ceramics from the yard can either be pieced together or are similar to the floor fragments in building "o." Therefore it is indeed safe to conclude that some rather high quality ceramic items were used by slaves living in building "o." It would be logical to characterize these objects as hand-me-downs from the house—either outdated, damaged, or worn—or that they were stolen from the house. One could argue that some of these ceramics were never once used in the house at all but were actually bought by or for the slaves exclusively for use in the quarters.

That question too can be answered by archaeological evidence. A comparison of vessels found only in deposits from the mansion with the Mulberry Row vessels from the cabin and yard can help sort the possessions used exclusively by slaves from those used only in the house. For example, one might conclude that certain vessels may have been purchased for or by slaves if they show up in the cabin dirt floor and *do not* match any of the mansion fragments. Or it may be that certain vessels were mansion discards in the cabin yards if they match the mansion but not the cabin floor sherds. In the final analysis, however, practically *all* the refined tablewares from the house foundations matched those from cabin "o," indicating that slaves were furnished or furnished themselves from the house stores (fig. 46). Vessel types that did not match from house to quarter were primarily coarse earthenwares, utilitarian stoneware, and some early dated refined earthenware which could give some indication of a hand-me-down system.

FIGURE 46. *Assemblage of ceramics found along the foundations of the Monticello mansion arranged as found in association with the mansion plan, with similar ceramics found along Mulberry Row (inside house outline).*

While the separation of master/slave artifacts archaeologically seems in theory to be valid and enlightening, there are a number of variables that could distort the results. While determining when things were thrown around the house and building "o" can be unusually accurate, it could be that some hand-me-downs were used and thrown away in the cabin in the 1770s before the drain began to be filled after 1780. Consequently objects that were used earlier in the house and broken there were thrown somewhere else and never recovered archaeologically. Therefore, the fact that certain earlier cabin artifacts do not match samples from the house drain does not necessarily mean that they were materials only issued to or bought by slaves. Also, there is every reason to believe that slaves lived in the basement rooms of the house and therefore perhaps some of the drain objects may have belonged to them. Of course, determining the relative quality of the various types of Chinese porcelain from these sites and the degree to which they might reflect social and economic class structure was another key to discovering ownership.

As part of its policy to produce and sell reproductions of Jefferson-related objects, the Monticello gift shop contacted representatives of mainland Chinese potters who were, for obvious reasons, the prime candidates to reproduce Jeffersonian Chinese porcelain. On one occasion, the Chinese potters visited Monticello and asked to see the porcelain from the archaeological excavations. All of the archaeological porcelain was laid out, indiscriminately, without suggestion of who might have used the various pieces. The first reaction from the potters was one of horror. In translation, it was clear that some of what they saw reflected poorly on the taste and means of Mr. Jefferson. The underglazed blue floral plates, for example, were only "fit for servants in China," certainly not for the nobility of the stature of a President (see fig. 42). They were relieved to learn that those plates indeed came from the servants' house "o" along Mulberry Row. Since their visit, however, the same slave plates were found along the house foundation.

The Chinese potters' judgment of quality requires an explanation. Could the presence of that inferior pattern at the house be more evidence that slaves lived in the basement of the house, as the documents suggest? Probably so, and in fact, some of the fragments came from near the basement window adjacent to what may have been a domestic room. Alternatively, could these plates be more hand-me-downs? Possibly, but it is likely that like other Europeans or Americans, Jefferson took whatever was available from the Chinese manufacturers, who often sent much of what they considered inferior but good enough for their customers in the west. Finally, when he could order better quality, the plain blue and white vessels may well have gone to the slaves in the house and living at building "o."

In any event, our Chinese visitors were as impressed with other samples of the porcelain collection as they were disappointed in the plain blue plates. For example, in the potters' opinion Jefferson's polychrome overglazed set of teaware with the *Valentine* or *Altar of Love* pattern was deemed the "highest quality in China" and truly fit for the nobility. In the end the potters went away satisfied that a member of the American elite as distinguished as Thomas Jefferson was sophisticated enough to know his Chinese porcelain. Nevertheless, it is clear that good or bad quality ceramics do not necessarily define the status of their users nor do they necessarily directly reflect taste.

The slave diet is another and perhaps more telling indication of standard of living. A considerable quantity of butchered animal bones from the occupation level of building "o" suggest a less affluent but not a poor diet.[2] Although many of the bones were from poorer cuts of meat, the great number of long bones from the same collection tends to suggest a richer diet. Yet a number of the bones were split up considerably with powerful blows, some of the elements sawn into small pieces, and some of the bones show marks that strongly indicate that meat was stripped from the bone with a knife. The whole fragmentation process suggests that the meat was used primarily in stews. However, the long bones show that the bill of fare had some variety; cow and pig remains about equal in quantity. Similarly, the presence of several deer bones from quarter "o" indicates some variety as well (fig. 47). On the other hand, rodent gnaw marks on some of the bones show that, although slaves may have eaten relatively well using surprisingly fine ceramics, the dinner conditions may have been unsanitary.

The fact that many of the bones, gnawed and otherwise, were found in the

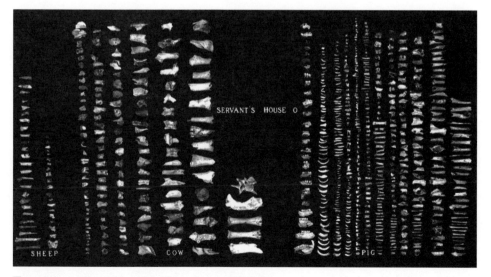

FIGURE 47. *Faunal remains from slave cabin "o."*

fill in the cellar, directly beneath the living areas, paints a dismal picture of sanitation. It should be pointed out, however, that the question of where the material came from, mansion or quarter, exists with the animal bone just as it does with the ceramics. Unlike the ceramics, the bones cannot be mended from feature to feature or site to site. And, since no bone was found along the house foundation, a good case may be made that the bones from Mulberry Row are a hopeless mix from both Jefferson's table and the occupants of building "o." Nonetheless, it is clear that slaves ate far better than documentary account books suggest.

Along with the garbage and trash, the root cellar and the rest of the occupation level at building "o" contained a number of buttons. The collection, numbering forty in all, included a variety of button types—plated brass, pewter, brass-faced bone, and bone. The number and variety of buttons may be the clues to an explanation of their presence. According to oral tradition, female slaves traditionally made heavy quilts from clothes discarded by the master's family, the cutting and sewing done at night in front of the hearth in the quarters. It follows that the fabrication of quilts from the old shirts and coats might result in the ultimate discard near the hearth of a great number and variety of buttons rendered useless by the new use for the cloth. It would have been convenient to throw the rejected buttons into the cellars or by the same token many could have filtered down into the cellars through cracks between the floor boards. Of course, slaves also made most of their own clothes and the buttons may mark that activity as well.

A total of 910 ceramic vessels were found in major occupation soil layers of building "s" and "t" and buried in the border beds of the garden at the bottom of the slope behind the house sites, together giving a range of occupation of ca. 1790–1830 (see Appendix A, figs. 67–69). The assemblage included matched teaware sets in polychrome handpainted pearlware and Chinese porcelain. There was also a wide variety of form—over thirty-four different vessel shapes in all. A large number of wine bottles (236) and drinking glasses (sixty-one tumblers) were also found.

The same "r," "s," and "t" site produced a revealing collection of butchered animal bones, most found in the garden border bed below building "s" where the bulk of the domestic refuse was thrown. The specimens were generally extremely fragmentary, probably indicating that the beef, pork, and fowl meat primarily went

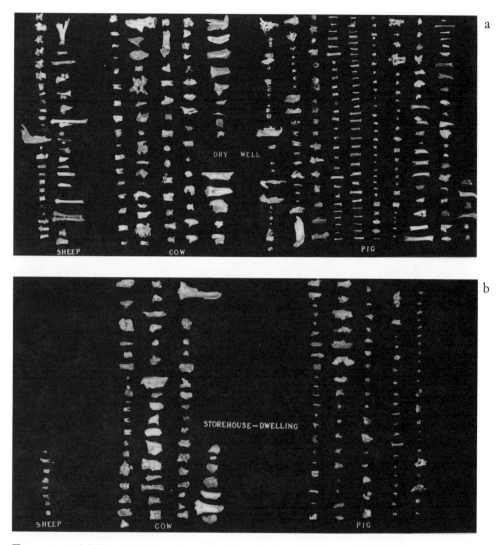

FIGURE 48. *(a) Identified faunal remains from the dry well: presumably from the table at the mansion. (b) Identified faunal remains from the "storehouse-dwelling." Note the extremely fragmented condition of these bones, as well as the almost total absence of sheep bones, indicating a distinct difference in diet.*

into stews. Stew is also indicated by the fact that much of the meat, particularly the pork, was from the least meaty parts of the animals.

Even sites identified on the 1796 insurance plat as utility outbuildings, such as building "l," the storehouse, and at the two ends of building "m," the smokehouse/dairy, produced a great number of domestic artifacts indicating domestic use as well. For example, 181 ceramic vessels in eighteen forms were recovered from the so-called storehouse along with an extensive collection of food bones. The faunal remains from the deposits show that whoever was living in the storehouse was eating primarily stews, as the bones were extremely fragmentary and the cuts of meat were primarily of the poorest quality.

If the adage "we are what we eat" is true, then comparative analysis of the butchered animal bones from the sites of the slave houses and mansion alike should show variation in diet and perhaps relative wealth and social standing (figs. 48a and 48b). As one might expect, the analysis did show that the highest percentages of the best cuts of meat were found in a deposit near the mansion (dry well), but the analysis also showed that some slaves along Mulberry Row ate better than others. The slaves living in building "t" and building "o" for example, consumed the better cuts of meat, while the occupants of building "s" and the storehouse were eating the less meatier parts of the animals ground up for stew. Although pork dominates the Mulberry Row sites and the dry well near the house, it is obvious that the better, more tender and meaty body parts of the pigs (as well as the cattle) were served in the Monticello house. And relatively absent from the dry well collection is the great number of non-identifiable bones, literally pulverized in processing, suggesting that unlike the quarters, stews were not much a part of meals in the house. Sheep were also a much higher percentage of the number of animals found in the dry well as compared to the bones found at the storehouse and building "o" suggesting that mutton was probably considered a delicacy primarily for the house table. On the other hand, during the 1790s Jefferson began raising sheep exclusively for slave rations.

Archaeologists studying plantations in coastal Georgia and northern Florida[3] have done a functional analysis of ceramics from the sites of what they have termed "planter, overseer, and slave." They postulated that differences in the diets of the three groups would be reflected in the relative numbers of plates normally used for serving the better meat cuts while bowls were the obvious requirement for stew. The data from those southern sites worked out precisely as the archaeologists predicted; many more hollowware to flatware from the slave site, a balance of the two from the overseer, and a distinct predominance of flatware from the planter's house.

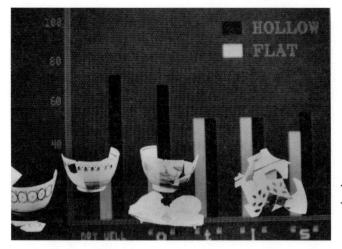

Figure 49. *Comparison of flat to hollow wares from five sites along Mulberry Row: dry well, buildings "o," "t," "l," and "s."*

The same kind of test at Monticello had quite different results, even though the animal bones found (as shown above) indicated that roasts and chops went on the table in the house more frequently than they appeared in the slave quarters. Of the bowls and plates found on the five sites, the hollow-to-flat ratio varied considerably ranging from close to even, to about 1:4 with plates always predominating (fig. 49). In fact, the plates were greatest at the slave quarters, where the faunal analysis indicated a diet of a lesser quality. One can conclude that such comparisons are not at all valid reflections of diet or relative wealth, at least at Monticello. Why?

The unexpectedly low percentages of ceramic plates in the archaeological deposits likely comprised of house artifacts could be explained by the fact that the plates in the house were made of pewter and/or silver, both rarely broken or discarded or lost. In fact, a study of a number of Albemarle probate inventories of the last thirty years of the eighteenth century shows that pewter plates were the predominant serviceware of most people, and particularly for the middle or upper classes.[4] There is every reason to assume that Jefferson had as much or more of the metal vessels than his neighbors.

It is clear that both metal flatware and diet were status symbols. The custom of tea drinking as a symbol of wealth or social standing by the late eighteenth century is more problematic. A description of the interior of a slave house in nineteenth-century Mississippi suggests that slave cabins often contained, among other amenities, the proper tea/coffee ware.

FIGURE 50. *The three common styles of English transfer-printed pearlware from the Monticello excavations.*

> In ... [slave cabins] there was a show of neatness and luxury; cup-
> boards of Blue Liverpool Ware, coffee mills, looking glasses, tables,
> chairs, trunks and chests of as good clothes as I clothe myself or
> Family. . .[5]

It should also be pointed out that the use of and symbolic meaning of drinking tea changed through time, slipping in prestige. By the last quarter of the eighteenth century tea had also become the drink of the urban working poor.[6]

Regardless of who was drinking tea at Monticello, in 1791 Thomas Jefferson's daughter, Martha, revealed the source of what became many of these fragmented teawares along Mulberry Row.

> ... not relying on the carefulness of the boys [slave waiters] [she] ...
> took an account of the plate china &c. and locked up all that was not
> in immediate use ... except our beautiful cups which being obliged to
> leave out [as they] are all broke but one.[7]

FIGURE 51. *Rare United States silver half dime, 1797. Perhaps one made at the Philadelphia mint to fill Jefferson's 1797 order for $300 worth of half dimes (size = 16.5 mm).*

A partial inventory of house furnishings made soon after Jefferson's death in 1826 gives some hints about the identity of ceramics he might have owned. Prominent on the list are Blue Liverpool cups, bowls, tureens, and plates. Blue Liverpool became a generic name for blue underglazed transfer-printed English pearlware. Conspicuous in late Jefferson period archaeological deposits are two patterns of that ware: vessels with pastoral scenes and borders of what became known as the "wild rose" pattern and plates, platters, tureens, and serving bowls decorated with a floral-like pattern of "pinwheels" and "sunflowers" with a central floral panel (figs. 41 and 50). Either (or perhaps both) of these might be broken pieces from the Blue Liverpool set listed in the inventory. Elements of both the transfer-printed designs appear to reflect design features that Jefferson found appealing elsewhere. The ceiling pattern, for example, of the Roman Temple of Vesta is strikingly similar to the "pinwheels" and "sunflowers," and the landscape scenes on the wild rose pattern vessels depict the picturesque English landscape that Jefferson so admired.

Other objects reflect Jefferson's interests and the family more directly: a United States 1797 one-half dime (fig. 51), a glass wine bottle seal bearing the name of the famous French winery Chateau la Fite (fig. 52), and a seal bearing a stylized "R" for what is almost certainly the family of Jefferson's son-in-law, Randolph (fig. 53). Jefferson felt that a country should have a good supply of small change which would hold down the prices of

FIGURE 52. *Glass wine bottle seal bearing the logo of Chateau la Fite winery, Bordeaux (diameter = 3.2 cm).*

FIGURE 53. *Randolph family (?) signet for sealing wax.*

small articles and he devised the United States decimal monetary system. In 1797, he sent $300 to the Franklin mint to be converted into half dimes, one of which he paid the slave, Wormley, for cleaning the well in 1797. Jefferson was also interested in viticulture and ordered 600 bottles of Chateau la Fite wine from France in 1784 but later complained that it never arrived. The seal proves, however that at least one bottle made it to Monticello.

From Free Laborers

The house site of William Stewart and later Elisha Watkins with its tight period of documented occupation (1800-1809) yielded a significant collection of objects presumably reflecting the lifestyle of Monticello's free artisans. Like the quarters and house, ceramics make up the bulk of the collection and include a minimum of 125 vessels, primarily of English creamware and pearlware but also including some Chinese porcelain. In fact, fragments of the so-called slave Chinese porcelain so common on Mulberry Row and even fragments of the *Altar of Love* were found on the Stewart/Watkins site as well. Some of the creamware showed extreme wear indicating a certain degree of poverty; and, significantly there were many matched teaware sets found there as well as quantities of polychrome decorated pearlware. Some of the same polychrome pearlware forms and decoration were common on Mulberry Row but not so common in the collections from the house, perhaps indicating that this type of pottery was the folk ware of the laboring classes. On the other hand, the presence of porcelain matching the house and the slave quarters suggests that free laborers as well as slaves

FIGURE 54. *One of matching pair of Thomas Jefferson's pocket pistols from the Thomas Jefferson Memorial Foundation collection shown with iron loading wrench recovered near the site of the blacksmith's shop on Mulberry Row (length = 11.1 cm).*

either received second-hand items or took freely from the house stores.

Stewart's habitual drinking and the resulting erratic work record eventually led to his dismissal. While no great accumulation of bottle glass was found at this house, perhaps the presence of discarded unfinished iron implements and tools found in the cellar and yard is a reflection of his unsteady work style. The iron was potentially reusable and the tools were not broken.

FIGURE 55. *Tin cup from Mulberry Row, possibly the work of Isaac.*

From the Craft Shops

Besides the types of nails made in the nailery the excavations also recovered evidence of bone button, firearm, and tin manufacturing. The recovery of a pocket pistol wrench near the smith's shop suggests that the smiths may have made a replacement there (fig. 54).The flange of one of Jefferson's pocket pistols in the Monticello collections shows extreme wear, in fact, so much wear that the original wrench used to unscrew the barrel for loading probably no longer fit. It is likely that the obsolete original is the one recovered near the smith's shop. Other firearms parts included various parts from firing mechanisms and backplates, which indicate that gun repairs were made in the Mulberry Row shop. Finally a tin cup recovered near the storehouse for iron may have been made by Isaac, who apprenticed as a tinsmith in Philadelphia (fig. 55).

From the Garden

Few but significant garden-related artifacts were also recovered during the excavations (fig. 56). Fragments of bottomless salt-glazed stoneware pots and lids were found on the slope between the Mulberry Row buildings.

Archival research located a letter referencing Jefferson's order of sea kale pots from Wickham from Richard Randolph's pottery near Richmond in 1821.[8] Sea kale for the table grows best in darkness, so it is probable that these bottomless vessels once shaded Jefferson's sea kale crops. Unstratified fragments from a notched rim unglazed flower pot were also found but it is uncertain if the pot dates to the Jefferson period. This rim form, however, matches fragments unearthed at Mount Vernon. More flower pot fragments, which may be early nineteenth century French in origin with neo-classical rouletting, were also found, most in post-Jefferson strata. Also recovered were sherds of a German saltglazed stoneware *Blumenkübel*. The ceramics from the house drain included a number of fragments of three forms of Jefferson period flowerpots as well. Clearly they could have fallen from the window sill of the study or nearby greenhouse room.

FIGURE 56. *American saltglazed stoneware forcing pot used in the garden to tenderize certain vegetables such as sea kale. Jefferson ordered sea kale pots from the Randolph pottery near Richmond. These fragments may be from the pottery.*

Other garden furniture included sherds from what may be a gigantic terra cotta garden cistern, but again its archaeological context may be suggesting that this object was the property of later Monticello owners.

CHAPTER FOUR NOTES

[1] Edmund Bacon to Thomas Jefferson, 15 April 1808, 1 December 1808.

[2] D. Crader-Johnson, "Faunal Remains From Slave Quarter 'o' at Monticello." Paper presented at the Annual Meeting of Society for Historical Archaeology, Williamsburg, VA, 1984.

[3] See especially J. S. Otto, *Cannon's Point Plantation* (San Diego: Academic Press, 1984).

[4] Ann Smart, "The Role of Pewter as 'Missing Artifact': Evidence from Late Eighteenth-Century Probate Inventories, Albemarle County, Virginia." Paper Presented at the Annual Meeting of the Society for Historical Archaeology, Williamsburg, 1984.

[5] E. D. Genovese, *Roll Jordon Roll* (New York: Pantheon Books, 1974), 527.

[6] Barbara Carson, personal communication, 1991.

[7] J. A. Bear, Jr., ed., *The Family Letters of Thomas Jefferson* (Columbia: University of Missouri Press, 1966), 68.

[8] Edmund Peyton to Thomas Jefferson, 29 March 1821.

IN TOUCH WITH THE PAST

At first I could barely make out their shapes in the wispy morning fog, but the deafening roar and top-heavy profiles soon told me the usual United Parcel Service delivery truck convoy was coming onto U.S. Route 250 opposite Shadwell. I could not help thinking how much had changed since the young Thomas Jefferson had seen Monacan Indians on the same road.

It was 1993—the year Thomas Jefferson was commemorated on his 250th birthday and the year that Shadwell, his birthplace site so close to Monticello, was in its third season of fieldwork. I was there to open the Shadwell gate to let my archaeological colleagues and field school students drive up to the excavation. I had arrived early to provide some direction to the work, but my mind was definitely not on the Shadwell excavation on this day. I needed to write the conclusion to this book. When I reached the top of the hill my gaze turned west toward Monticello. I half-hoped that some sort of sign might appear on the horizon giving me the wisdom to see just what it was about Jefferson's world that all those years of archaeology at Monticello had discovered. But, alas, no handwriting in the sky.

Later that morning I found myself at the word processor. The word "experience" kept coming to me as I attempted to sum up archaeology's contribution to understanding Monticello. I have often thought that archaeology's ability to reach back across time and touch things last touched by people long dead is the nearest thing to time travel there is. That is, by uncovering things one soil layer at a time, it is almost possible to revisit the past. That may be "it," I thought. Archaeology presented the opportunity to revisit or re-experience Jefferson's Monticello world. For instance, because of archaeology we can envision Thomas Jefferson, the scientist, experimenting with his microscope on his window sill. Or, we can walk along Mulberry Row and picture the slave, Isaac, expertly putting the finishing touches on a tin cup, or the blacksmith, William Stewart, testing a renovated gun. Visitors can now more completely experience and understand the Monticello that nestles within the greater landscape design of its builder, who made a rugged mountaintop conform to his ideas of controlled space and ornament. With archaeology fleshing out the documentary story, we can experience the heroic scale of Jefferson's terraced garden and appreciate that its construction required as much digging, filling, leveling, and retaining as a modern shopping center. Of equal importance, it has been archaeology that has helped erase the false impression that Monticello was a house only, with Jefferson, like some kind of learned monk in seclusion, literally looking down on the rest of the world. Foundations of scores of other buildings, artifacts of the slave and free-labor community, and the traces of an energetic landscape testify otherwise.

In part because of the archaeological experience along Mulberry Row, visitors today can go on a Plantation Community tour, where archaeology along Mulberry Row has made the physical evidence of slavery so visible. The grassy hillside no longer hides the testimony of slaves' pottery, glass, tools, implements, and the foundations and cellars of their Mulberry Row houses and workshops. Visions of the kaleidoscopic lifestyle of Monticello's slaves suggested by the archaeology puts to rest many timeworn stereotypes. As visitors see the many things left in the ground by slaves, it is easier to understand that despite the tremendous handicap of captivity, African-American people created a community at Monticello that was as intricate and vibrant as any other segment of colonial and early American society.

Can there be any doubt how Jefferson himself would feel knowing that we can understand his Monticello by the very archaeological process he first discovered? Can there be any doubt that, like Jefferson, we can be just as excited as that eight-year-old pioneer boy the first time his thoughts turned to digging for the past?

APPENDIX

The illustrations that follow are measured drawings of representative artifacts from the Monticello artifact study collection. Wherever possible, the captions include the place of manufacture and the study collection (S.C.) number. The order of the illustrations was determined primarily by the materials from which the object was made and the specific site at Monticello where the object was found. The master catalogue is held at the Department of Archaeology, Monticello.

FIGURE 57. *ENGLISH CREAMWARE: a. platter, deep yellow feather-edge S.C. 198; CHI-NESE PORCELAIN: b. saucer, red, white, gilt, overlgaze S.C. 624; ENGLISH CREAMWARE: c. fruit-basket, Leeds, S.C. 266; d. tea bowl, "bead and reel" rim S.C. 210; e. saucer "bead and reel" Staffordshire, S.C. 200; f. CHINESE PORCELAIN, bowl, blue un-derglaze, overglaze enamel, S.C. 564. All from DRY WELL deposit, 1770-1771.*

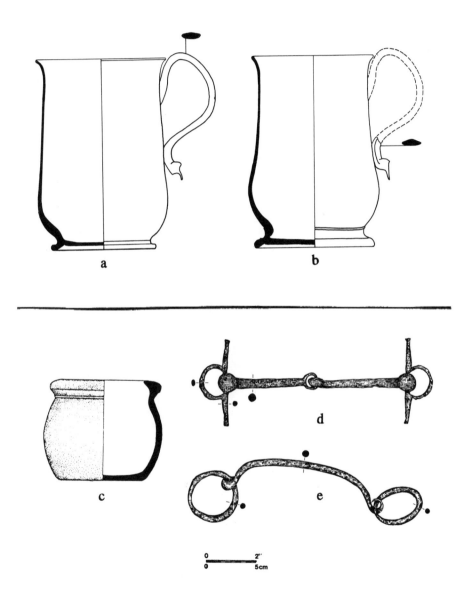

FIGURE 58. *STONEWARE: a. tankard, English white salt-glazed, S.C. 503; b. tankard, English white salt-glazed, S.C. 502; c. jar, English brown, salt-glazed, S.C. 7; IRON EQUESTRIAN HARDWARE: d. snaffle bit, S.C. 1283; e. bridoon, S.C. 128. All from DRY WELL deposit, 1770–1771, HOUSE.*

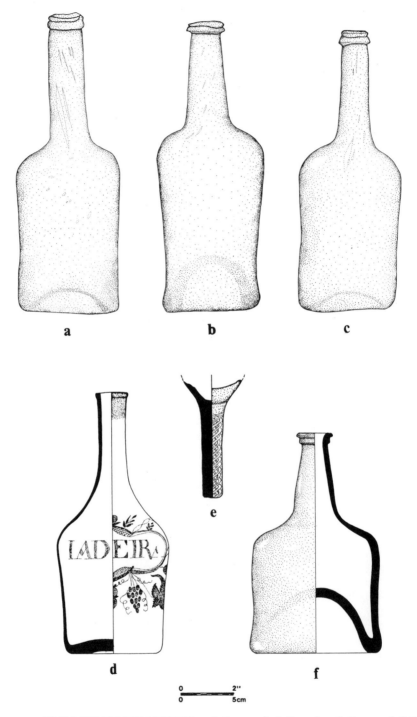

FIGURE 59. *ENGLISH WINE BOTTLES: a. S.C. 1522; b. S.C. 1528; c. S.C. 1522; d. DE-CANTER, clear, wheel-engraved [M]"ADEIR"[A] S.C. 1417; e. STEMWARE, clear, air twist S.C. 1376; f. ENGLISH WINE BOTTLE, S.C. 1523. All from DRY WELL deposit, 1770–1771.*

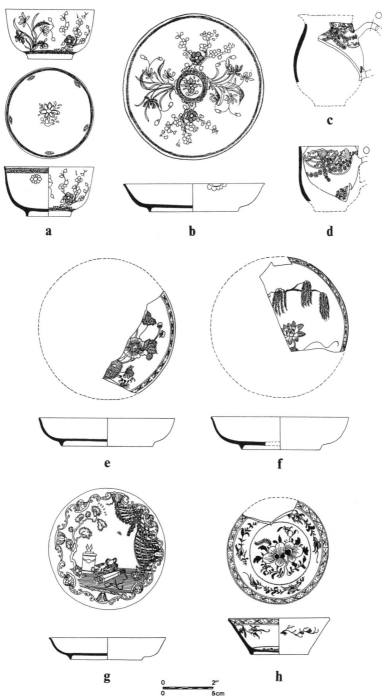

FIGURE 60. *CHINESE PORCELAIN: a. teabowl, blue underglaze, red, green, and gilt overglaze, one of seven matching tea bowls and saucers, S.C. 550; b. saucer blue underglaze, red, green, and gilt overglaze, S.C. 550; c. cream ewer polychrome "Altar of Love/Valentine" pattern, matches d. and e. All from GARDEN WALL deposit, 1808.*

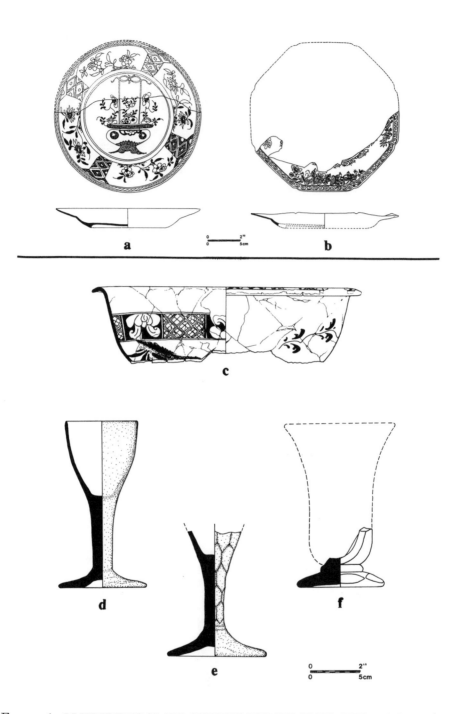

FIGURE 61. *BLUE UNDERGLAZE CHINESE PORCELAIN PLATES: a. S.C. 550; b. blue underglaze, rose, green, yellow overglaze, S.C. 550; c. ENGLISH DELFT, blue painted, S.C. 550; STEMWARE: d. S.C. 550; e. S.C. 550; f. DESSERT/JELLY GLASS, S.C. 550. All from the GARDEN WALL deposit, 1808.*

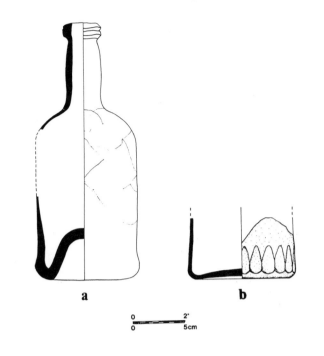

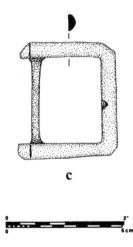

FIGURE 62. *a. WINE BOTTLE, S.C. 550; b. DECANTER BASE, clear, engraved "foot rim," S.C. 550; c. HARNESS BUCKLE, brass, S.C. 1799. All from GARDEN WALL deposit, 1808.*

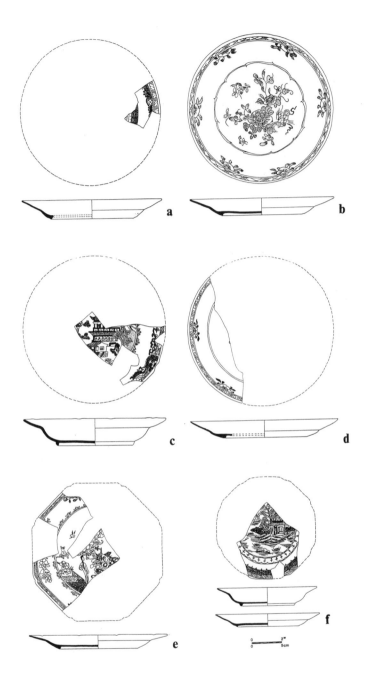

FIGURE 63. *BLUE UNDERGLAZE CHINESE PORCELAIN PLATES: a. S.C. 515; b. one of 15, ca. 1770-1790, Shaouking S.C. 505; c. blue underglaze, S.C. 253; d. blue underglaze, S.C. 511; e. blue underglaze, rose, green, yellow overglaze, S.C. 526; f. two separate dessert plates shown, (above) and (middle) profile S.C. 516, below, S.C. 517. All from SLAVE QUARTER "o", deposited ca. 1770-1810.*

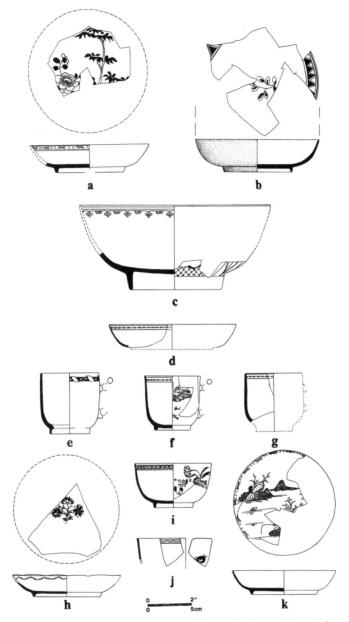

FIGURE 64. *a. CHINESE PORCELAIN saucer, blue underglaze, S.C. 558; b. ENGLISH PEARLWARE saucer, painted mustard yellow, ca. 1795-1815, S.C. 396; c. CHINESE PORCELAIN bowl, red and gilt overglaze, S.C. 624; CHINESE PORCELAIN: d. saucer, painted overglaze black, S.C. 593; CUPS: e. black overglaze, S.C. 592; f. black overglaze "o", S.C. 594; g. black overglaze, h. SAUCER, green underglaze, S.C. 621; CUPS: i. red, green, and gilt overglaze exterior red, green overglaze interior, S.C. 660; j. blue underglaze exterior, red overglaze rim interior, E.R. 410AD k. SAUCER, blue underglaze, S.C. 621. All from SLAVE QUARTER "o", deposited ca. 1770-1810.*

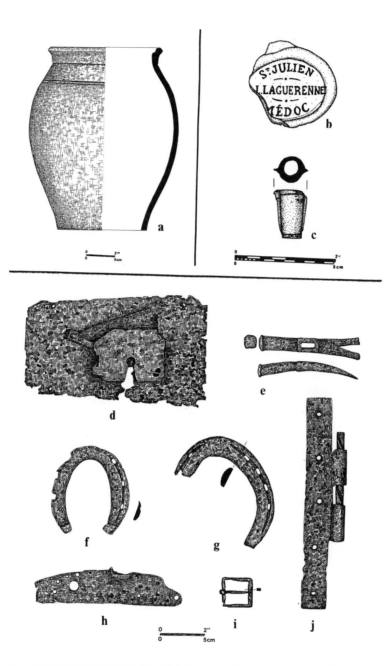

Figure 65. *a. STONEWARE JAR, English, brown salt-glazed, S.C. 72; b. GLASS BOTTLE SEAL, French, green, "ST. JULIEN L. LAGUERENNE MEDOC" from a 1793 Jefferson order of 504 bottles called, "a Medoc of 1788," S.C. 1501; c. FERELL, brass, S.C. 2291; IRON: d. stock lock, S.C. 1243; e. tack hammer, S.C. 1047; f. pony shoe, S.C. 1309; g. horseshoe, S.C. 1306; h. gun lockplate, stamped "E" exterior, ca. 1750, S.C. 1277; i. harness buckle, S.C. 1294; j. hinge, spiral "rising" type, S.C. 1108. All from the SLAVE QUARTER "o", deposited ca. 1770–1810.*

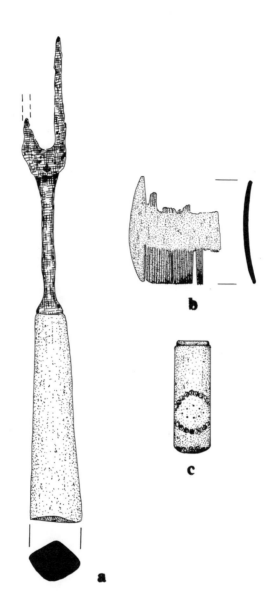

FIGURE 66. *a. FORK, bone handle, S.C. 1530; b. COMB, bone, S.C. 1548; c. PIN CASE, bone, S.C. 1563. All from SLAVE QUARTER "o", deposited ca. 1770–1810.*

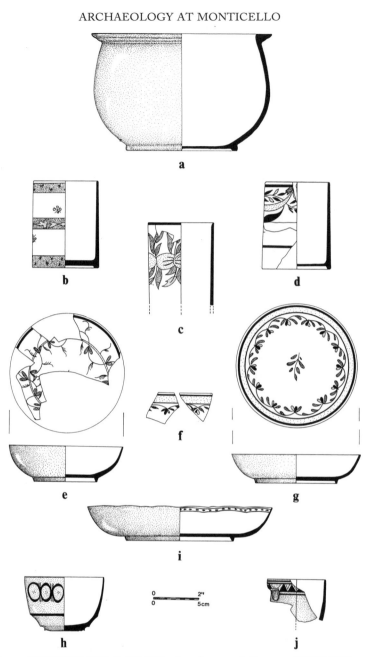

FIGURE 67. *a. ENGLISH CREAMWARE, chamber pot, S.C. 2200; ENGLISH PEARLWARE: b. MUG, brown, olive, and mustard yellow, S.C. 2126; c. MUG, olive, green, blue, yellow, and mustard yellow, S.C. 2102, d. MUG, yellow, green, olive, and mustard yellow, S.C. 2098; e. SAUCER, green, olive, and mustard yellow, S.C. 2125; f. TEA BOWL, yellow, green, brown, blue, and mustard yellow, S.C. 2230; g. SAUCER, painted brown, blue, green, and mustard yellow ca. 1795–1815, S.C. 381; h. TEA BOWL, blue, S.C. 2118; i. CHINESE PORCELAIN, dish, red, green overglaze rim band, S.C. 2182; j. ENGLISH PEARLWARE, cup painted mustard yellow, S.C. 2348. All except g. from SLAVE QUARTER "r", "s", "t", deposited 1808–1825.*

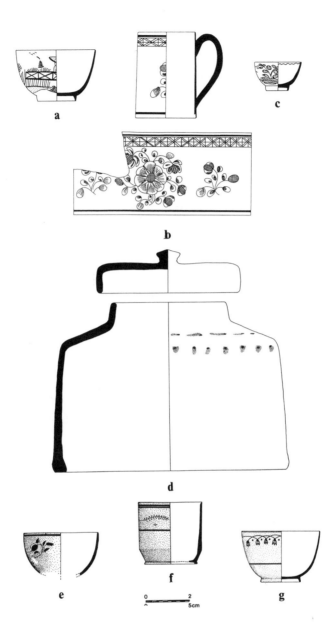

FIGURE 68. *ENGLISH PEARLWARE: a. CUP, painted blue, green, olive, mustard yellow, S.C. 2096; b. MUG, painted blue, S.C. 2092; c. MINIATURE CUP, painted blue, S.C. 2338; d. STONEWARE BLANCHING POT AND LID, salt-glazed, blue dashes, American, Richard Randolph pottery (?) near Curles Neck, Virginia, Jefferson 1821-22 order (?), S.C. 2136, 2152, ENGLISH PEARLWARE: e. tea bowl, painted blue, S.C. 2128; f. cup, painted blue, S.C. 2106; g. CUP, painted blue, S.C. 2093. All from SLAVE QUARTER "r", "s", "t", deposited 1808-1825.*

FIGURE 69. *a. CHINESE PORCELAIN PLATE, blue underglaze, S.C. 2184; b. ENGLISH PEARLWARE MUG, painted blue, S.C. 2127; c. FRENCH FAIENCE OINTMENT POT, stenciled exterior red overglazed letters: "Teiſfier Pfm Rue de Richelieu vis a vis le Café de Foi Paris". Label identifies pharmacist (?) (Teissier) and location of his shop (Richelieu Street) across from the (Café de Foi) in (Paris). Purchased by the servant, Gaspard, during Jefferson's stay at the Hotel d'Orléans on Rue de Richelieu "15 livres for shaving apparatus August 10, 1784". Café de Foi relocated to Palais Royale that same year, S.C. 2168, see also FIG. 29, p. 67; d. TURNER REFINED EARTHENWARE JUG, relief-molded hunting scene, S.C. 2129; ENGLISH WHITE SALT-GLAZED: e. salt or candle cup, S.C. 2144; f. toy tea bowl, S.C. 2144. All from SLAVE QUARTER "r", "s", "t", deposited 1808-1825.*

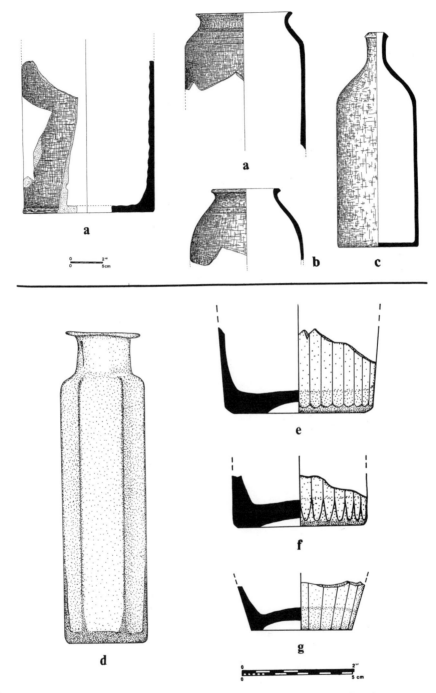

FIGURE 70. *ENGLISH BROWN SALT-GLAZED STONEWARE: a. jar rim and base, S.C. 2134; b. jar, S.C. 2147; c. ALBANY SLIP STONEWARE BOTTLE, S.C. 2168; d. PHARMACEUTICAL BOTTLE, light green, S.C. 2479; CLEAR GLASS TUMBLERS: e. S.C. 2383; f. S.C. 2415; g. S.C. 2418. All from SLAVE QUARTER "r", "s", "t", deposited 1808–1825.*

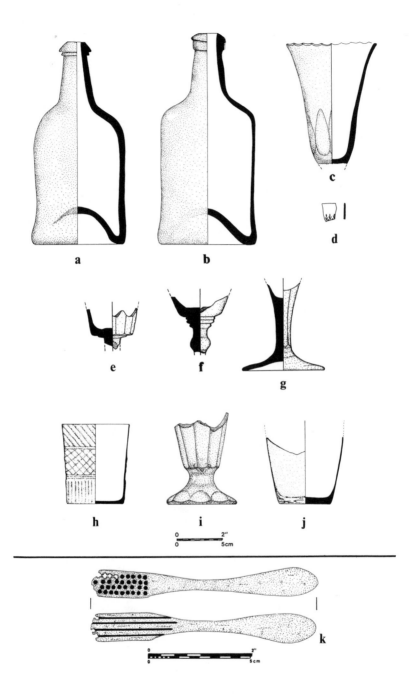

FIGURE 71. *ENGLISH WINE BOTTLES: a. S.C. 2070; b. S.C. 2071; DESSERT/JELLY GLASS, S.C. 2270; CLEAR STEMWARE: d. wheel-engraved, S.C. 2498; e. S.C. 2414; f. S.C. 2411; g. S.C. 2482; h. CLEAR GLASS TUMBLER, S.C. 2381; i. DESSERT/JELLY GLASS, S.C. 2376; j. CLEAR GLASS TUMBLER, S.C. 2416; k. TOOTHBRUSH, bone, S.C. 2261. All from SLAVE QUARTER "r", "s", "t", deposited 1808–1825.*

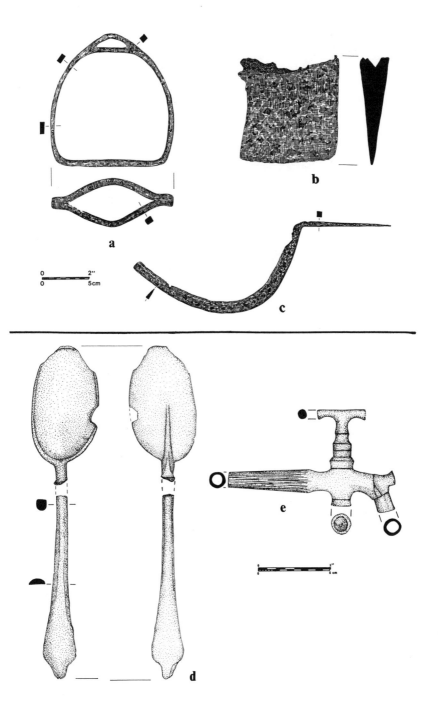

FIGURE 72. *IRON: a. stirrup, S.C. 1302; b. lath axe, S.C. 2580; c. sickle, S.C. 1075; PEW-TER: d. spoon bowl, S.C. 2314, handle; e. WHITE METAL: barrel tap, S.C. 1917. All from SLAVE QUARTER "r", "s", "t", 1808–1825.*

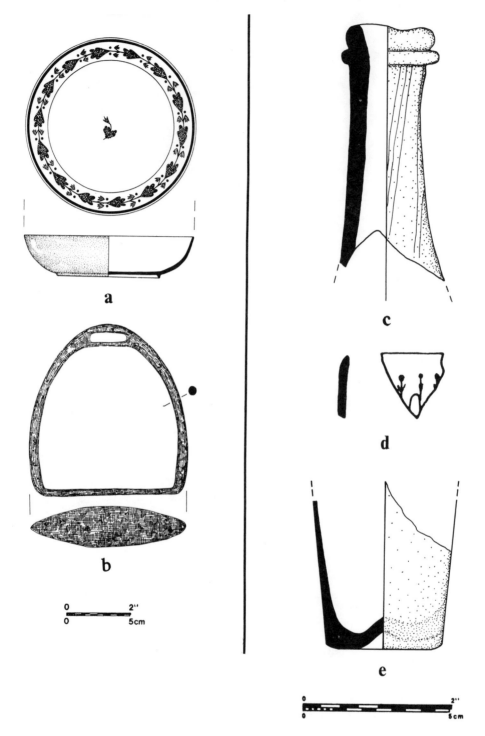

FIGURE 73. *a. SAUCER, brown, blue, green, and mustard yellow "I", S.C. 381; b. STIR-RUP S.C. 1301; c. FRENCH WINE BOTTLE "I", S.C. 1486; d. CLEAR STEMWARE wheel-engraved, S.C. 1364; e. S.C. 1409. All above from the STOREHOUSE BUILDING "I" site.*

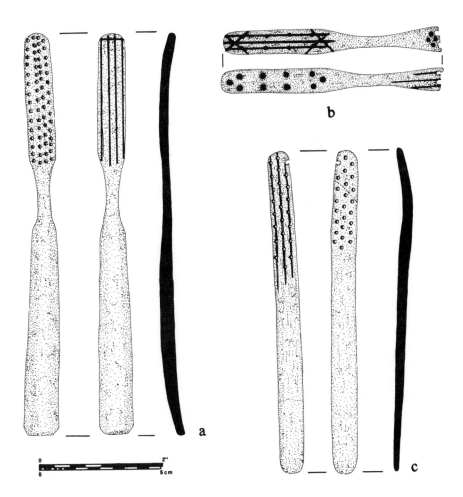

FIGURE 74. *From SMOKEHOUSE/DAIRY BUILDING "m". BONE TOOTH BRUSHES: a. S.C. 1550; b. S.C. 1554; c. S.C. 1553.*

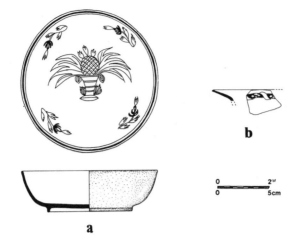

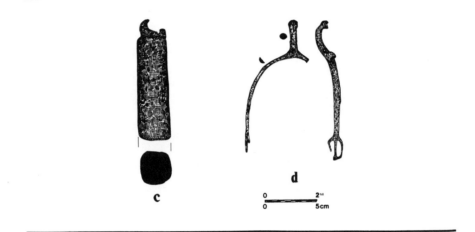

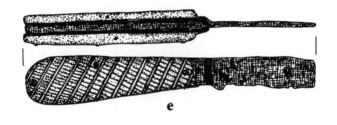

FIGURE 75. *a. ENGLISH PEARLWARE saucer, pineapple motif, painted brown, green, and mustard yellow, S.C. 399; b. CHINESE PORCELAIN plate, overglaze black, S.C. 590; c. SASH (?) WEIGHT, S.C. 1127; d. IRON SPUR, silver–plated, S.C. 1300; e. IRON CLASP KNIFE, bone handle, S.C. 1542. All from the SMOKEHOUSE/DAIRY BUILDING "m".*

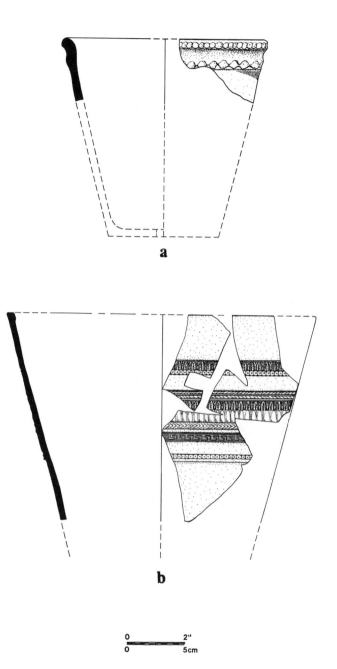

FIGURE 76. *a. COARSE-EARTHENWARE FLOWER POT, American (?) pot with simi-
lar rim form in archaeological collections at Washington's Mount Vernon, S.C. 13; b.
COARSE EARTHENWARE FLOWER POT, French (?), S.C. 15, 17, 18. From the
SMOKEHOUSE/DAIRY BUILDING "m".*

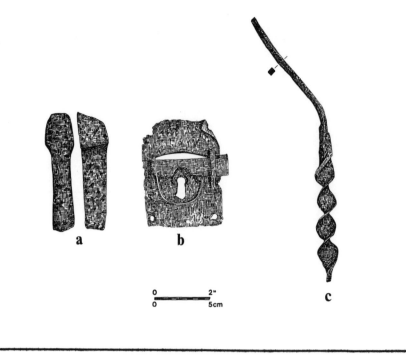

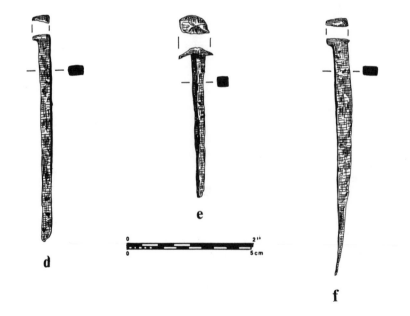

FIGURE 77. *a. IRON NAIL HEADING HARDY, S.C. 1026; b. IRON STOCK LOCK, S.C. 1240; c. IRON DRILL BIT, S.C. 1061; all above from the NAILERY BULDING "j". IRON NAILS: d. S.C. 874; e. S.C. 854; f. S.C. 876. All above from the SMITH'S SHOP BUILDING "d".*

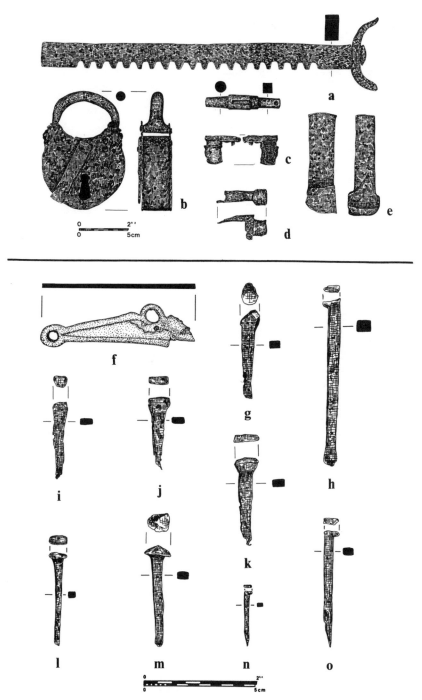

FIGURE 78. *IRON: a. carriage jack, S.C. 2066, and gear, S.C. 1318; b. padlock, S.C. 1254; c. gun powder pan, S.C. 1273; d. gun breech plug, S.C. 1272; e. nail heading hardy, S.C. 1027; f. musket sideplate, brass, stamped, S.C. 1802; IRON NAIL TYPES: g. S.C. 927; h. S.C. 872; i. S.C. 925; j. S.C. 924; k. S.C. 926; l. S.C. 849; m. S.C. 827; n. S.C. 860; o. S.C. 862. All from the NAILERY BUILDING "J".*

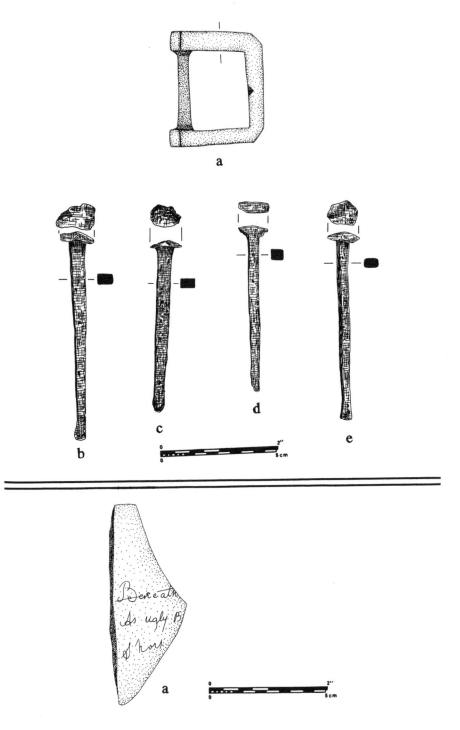

FIGURE 79. *a. BRASS HARNESS BUCKLE, S.C. 1800; IRON NAIL TYPES: c. S.C. 840; d. S.C. 837; e. S.C. 856; S.C. 838; all above from BUILDING "n". a. WRITING SLATE, inscribed: "Beneath ... As ugly B... Short..." S.C. 2005; from the JOINERY BUILDING "c".*

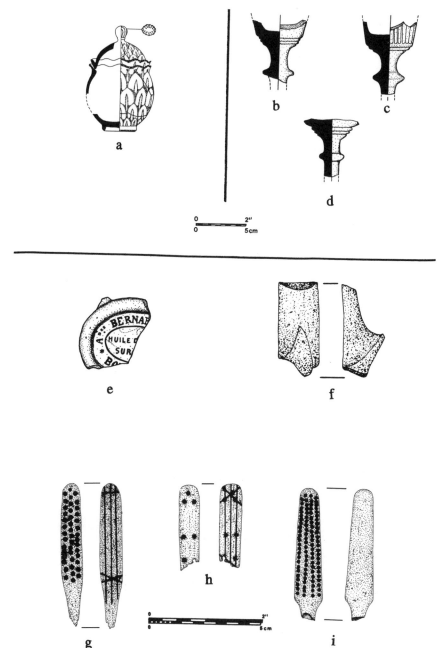

FIGURE 80. *a. CHINESE PORCELAIN CHOCOLATE POT, molded artichoke leaves, overglazed decoration, ca. 1760, te hua glaze, non-export quality (numerous other fragments suggest a number of these were used at Monticello), S.C. 648; CLEAR STEMWARE: b. S.C. 2545; c. S.C. 1394; d. S.C. 2604; e. GLASS BOTTLE SEAL, olive oil, light green embossed: "ADRE BERNAR ... HUILE D ... SUR ... BO ..." S.C. 1502; f. FIDDLE BOW "FROG", bone, S.C. 1564; BONE TOOTHBRUSHES: g. S.C. 1552; h. S.C. 1551; i. S.C. 2587. All from the KITCHEN YARD.*

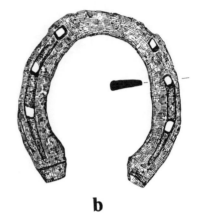
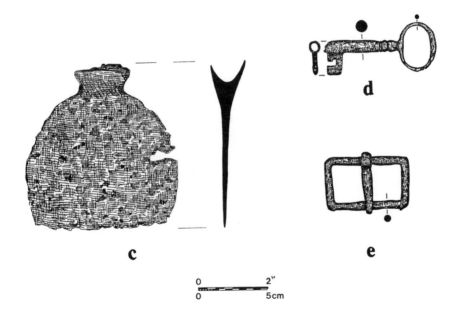

FIGURE 81. *IRON: a. scissors, S.C. 1210; b. horseshoe, S.C. 1303; c. shingling axe, S.C. 2310; d. key, S.C. 1270; e. harness buckle, S.C. 1298. All from the KITCHEN YARD.*

Glossary

Artifact: Any human made or human-altered object such as pottery, bottles, tools but also roads, fences, and entire landscape designs.

Backfill: The soil removed from an excavation unit, usually containing discarded artifacts, which is placed back into the unit from which it came upon completion of the work.

Dry well: A lined or unlined cellar dug deep enough into the ground to reach a constant cool temperature; usually for the cold storage of food.

Georgian Architecture: Architectural design ruled by symmetry whereby a central building block would be balanced by window and door openings and flanked by identical but smaller room elements; popular during the reigns of the Georgian kings of England.

Ha-ha: A fence-like barrier usually submerged below the near horizon in a landscape to protect planted areas from grazing animals yet not obstructing a picturesque view beyond; originally from the Latin, meaning "hedge."

Joinery: Woodworking shop along Mulberry Row where cabinetmakers manufactured furniture or other wooden objects requiring the joining together of wooden parts.

Plowzone: Layer of soil usually closest to the surface disturbed or "blended" by a plow during cultivation.

Posthole: A hole excavated during the installation of a post (usually to support a wooden fence) which leaves a stain in the soil that is archaeologically detectable long after the fence ceases to exist.

Postmold: A cavity in a posthole usually filled with soil created by the decay or removal of a post.

Roundabout: Thomas Jefferson's name for the concentric roads traveling through the Monticello landscape.

Transect: In archaeology, an experimental test excavation across some suspected buried cultural remnant, such as a road, trashpit, or terrace.

Vernacular Architecture: Folk building design, such as a log cabin.

Acknowledgements

Ten years or so of archaeological research at Monticello (1979-89) called for literally a cast of hundreds. Unfortunately, no matter how indebted I have become over those years for the toil and advice of so many others, I will not be able to adequately list them here. For those not mentioned I can only hope that their own feelings of accomplishment will be their just reward.

Appreciation must start with the sponsoring institution, The Thomas Jefferson Memorial Foundation, Inc., whose officers steadfastly recognized the need for the archaeological program, especially Dumas Malone (who, truth be known, finally admitted there was "some" value in digging), George Palmer, Virginius Shackelford, Lee Cochran, Wendell Garrett, Francis Berkeley, Howard Adams, and many others. James A. Bear, Jr., Charles Granquist, and Bill Beiswanger got the program going and took a chance that I just might find something. Help and "challenging advice" often came from Peter Hatch and historical advice from Cinder Stanton. Dan Jordan's tenure as Executive Director always encouraged the project, and it was he who showed the way to establishing one of the country's first student/teacher archaeological field schools.

Field supervisors Doug Sanford, Scott Shumate, Barbara Heath, and Susan Kern were invaluable record keepers and task masters and produced invaluable, insightful reports. Anna Gruber, Sondy Sanford, and Drake Patten did heroic and pioneering work in the lab as researchers as well as record keepers, and all contributed fine artwork and/or exhibit design. Thanks to Rachel Most, Derry Voysey, and Doug Wilson for shepherding this book through the proofing stages and Pat Valko for volunteer reference chasing.

To the over 150 field school students and teachers I express my deepest gratitude. And to my wife Ellen, son Marty, and daughter Libbey, for allowing me to let Charlottesville become our home town.